SCRIBBLE STONES ART GUIDE

Step-by-Step Painting Techniques and Tips to Spark Creativity!

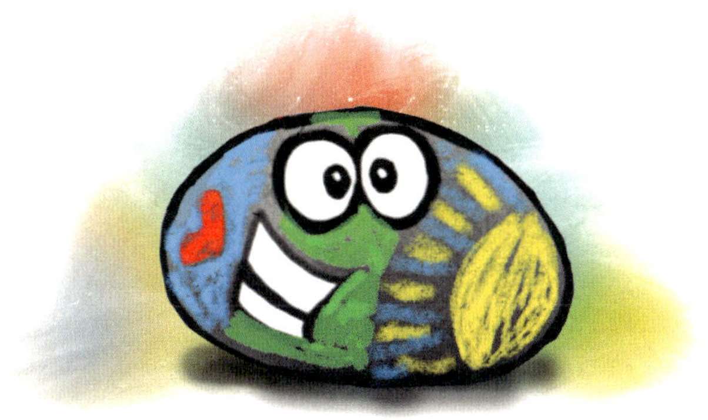

To my children, Ryan and Anna,

Who love to play with a giant stone pile in the backyard, which inspired the scribble stones story and art guide.

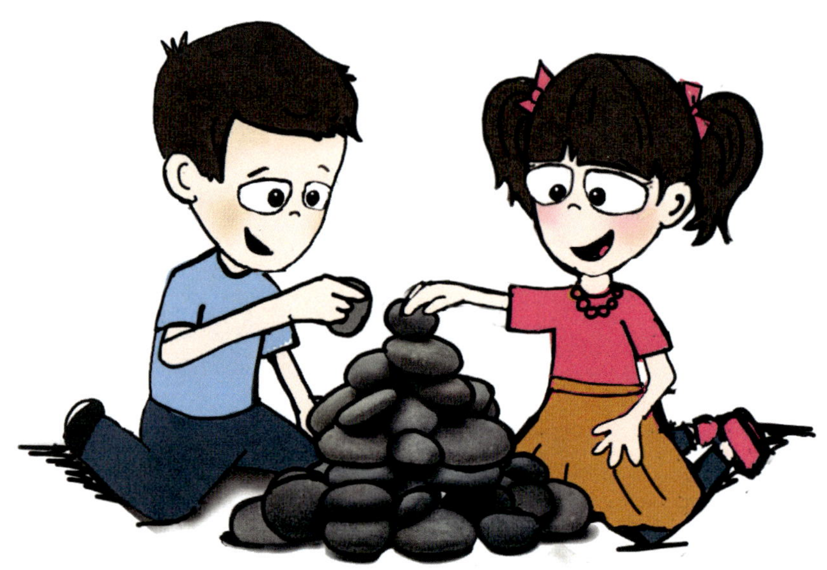

Copyright 2019 Diane Alber
All Rights Reserved
All inquiries about this book can be sent to the author at:
info@dianealber.com
Published in the United States by Diane Alber Art LLC
ISBN 978-1-7329346-5-8
Information or to book an event visit our website:
www.dianealber.com

Contents

Introduction

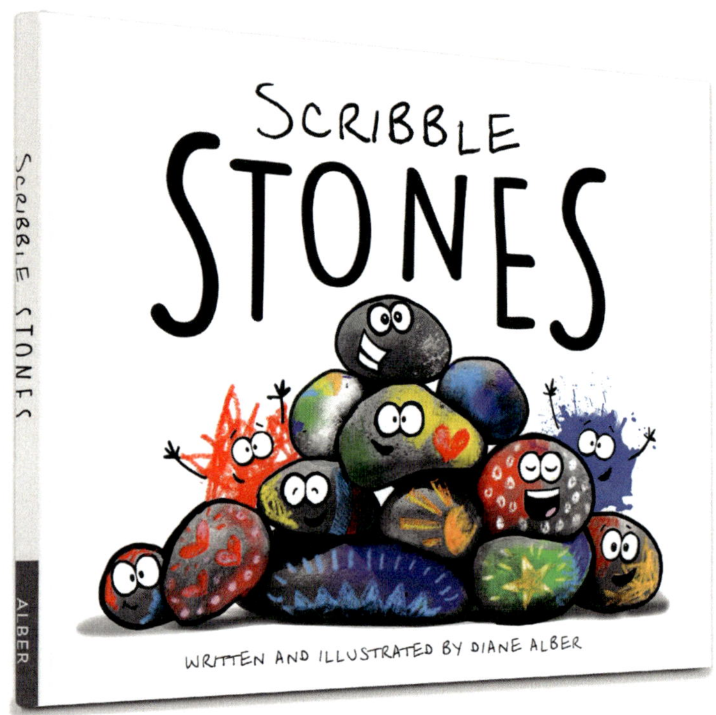

Scribble Stones Art Guide is a companion book to *Scribble Stones* by Diane Alber. *Scribble Stones* is about a little stone who wants nothing more than to bring happiness to the world, but instead ends up becoming a dull paperweight. He soon discovers that even though he didn't end up like he expected, he still has the power to bring happiness to the world, starting one kind act at a time.

Scribble Stone ART Project

Scribble stones are intended to inspire creativity and spread happiness through collaborative art.

HOW IT WORKS:

Find a stone and add some art,
a scribble, a splatter, or a happiness heart.
Then gift it away and let someone know
that this scribble stone makes happiness grow.
It's so very simple and easy to do.
Just add some more art and gift it away, too!

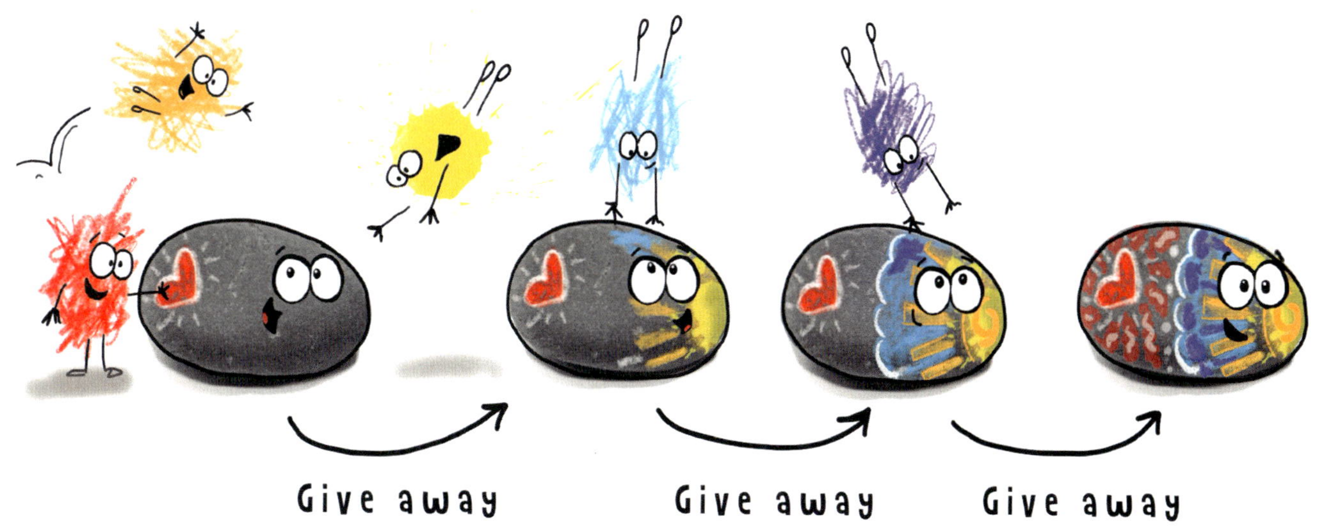

Once a stone is completed, find a happy home for it and start a new Scribble Stone! This is so much fun for friends, buddies, and classmates.

About the Author

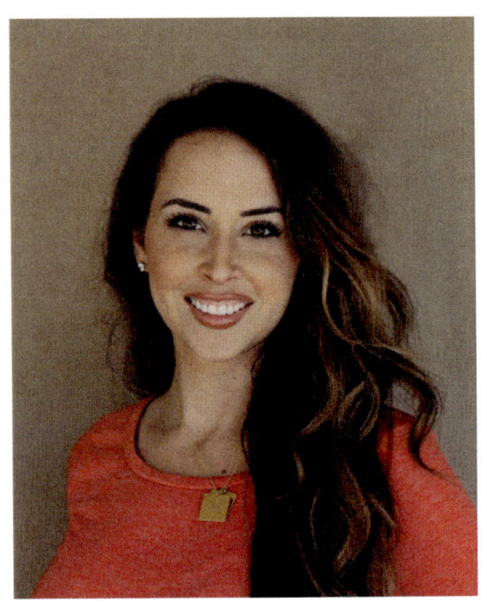

DIANE ALBER is the author and illustrator of the bestseller *I'm NOT just a Scribble....* She has had a passion for art since she held her first crayon at the age of two, which inspired her to earn a Bachelor's Degree in Fine Arts from Arizona State University. Diane lives in Chandler, Arizona with her husband and her two young children who love art. She plans on having several books in this series that will continue to encourage art and creativity. Find out more information by visiting: www.dianealber.com

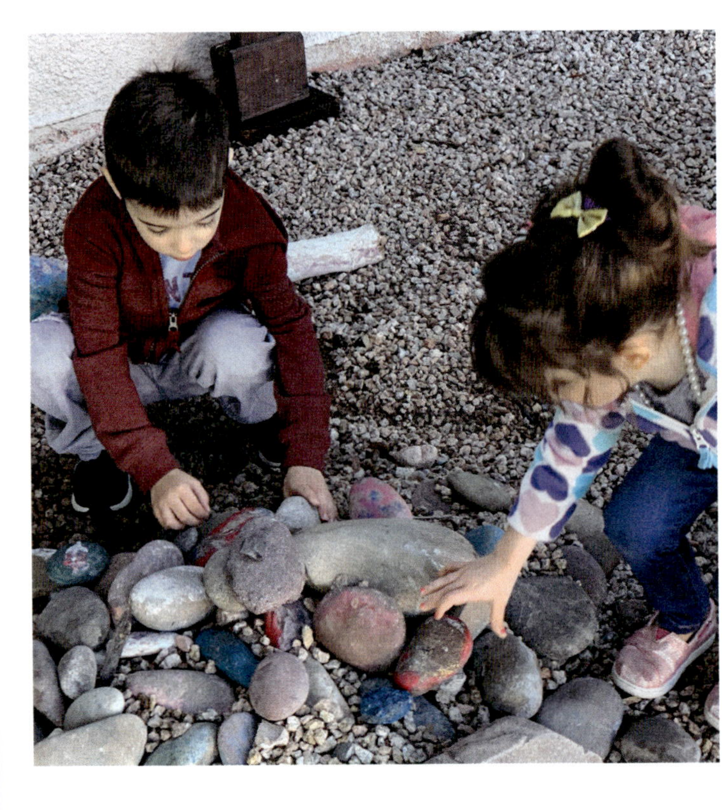

This rock pile inspired the Scribble Stones story!

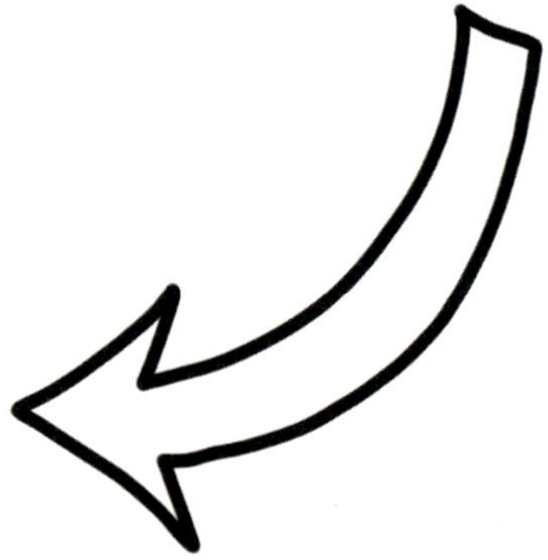

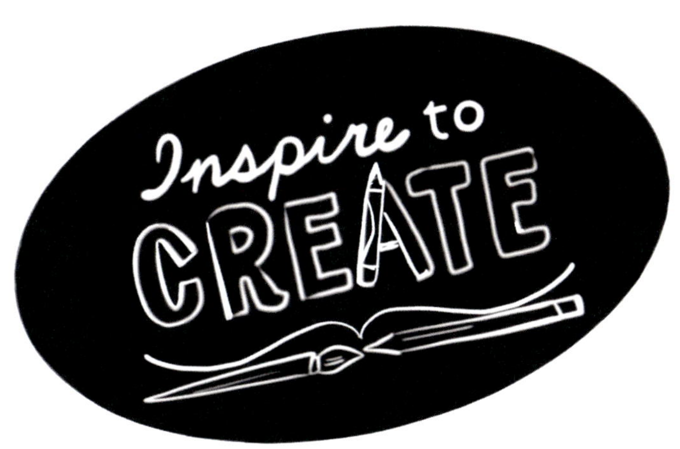

This series was written to inspire children to create!

Each of these books encourages children to use their fine motor skills, critical thinking skills, inventiveness, and language development. It also teaches them a valuable lesson in the process.

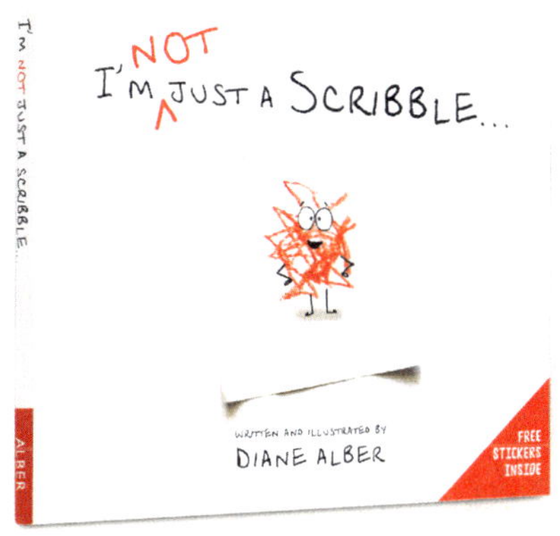

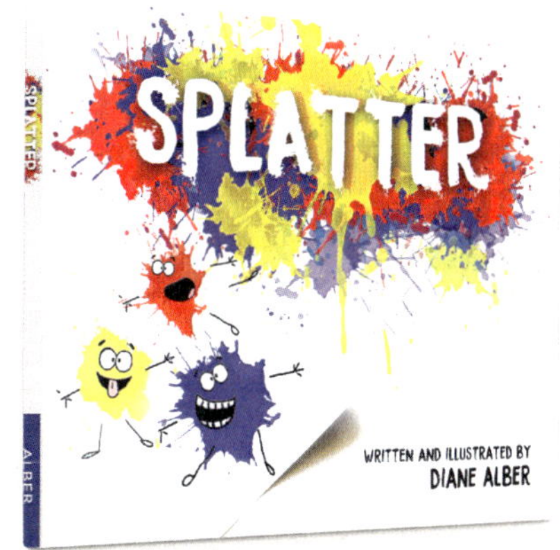

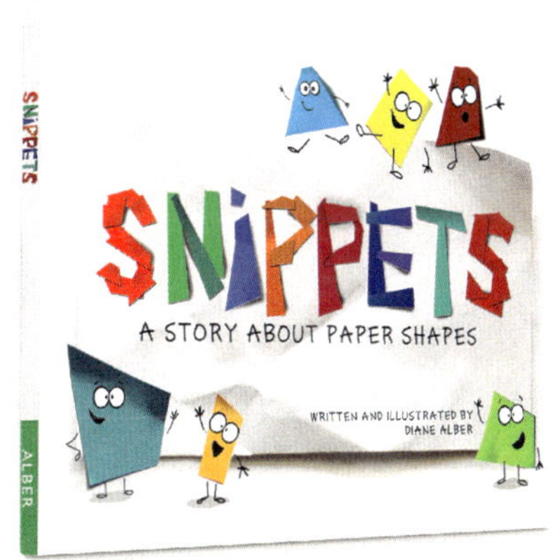

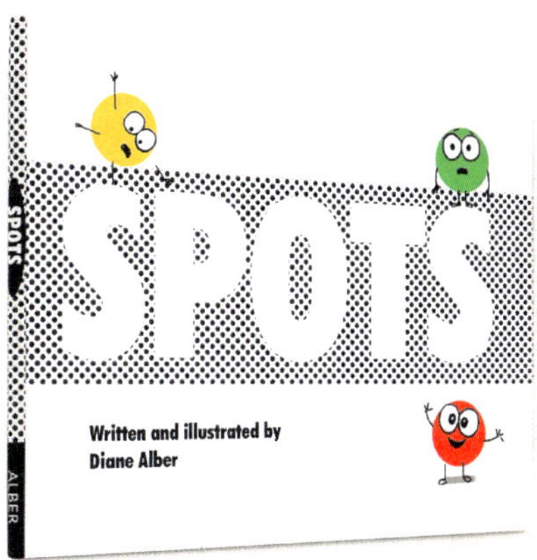

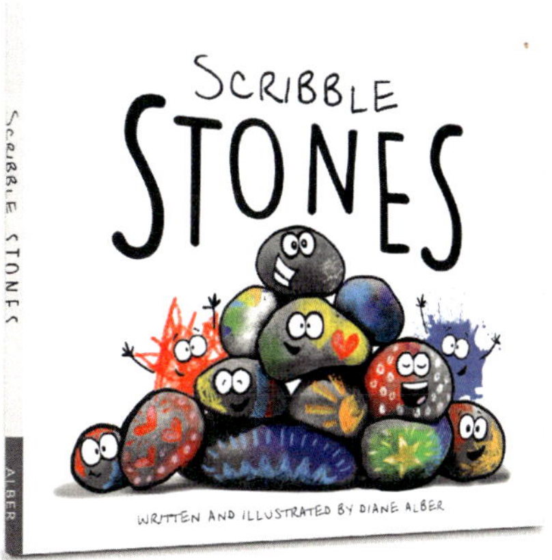

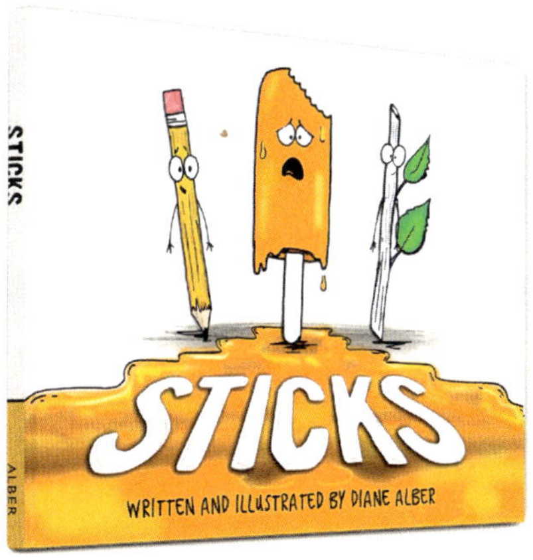

What Do You Need?

River rocks are the best stones to get. You can buy them online or at your local landscaping store.

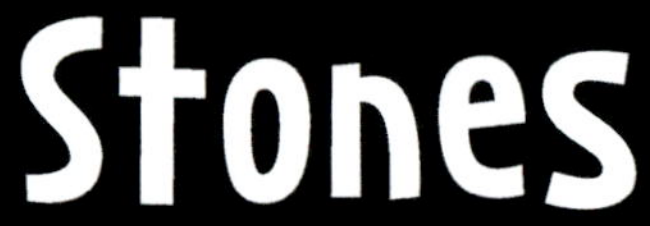

Stones

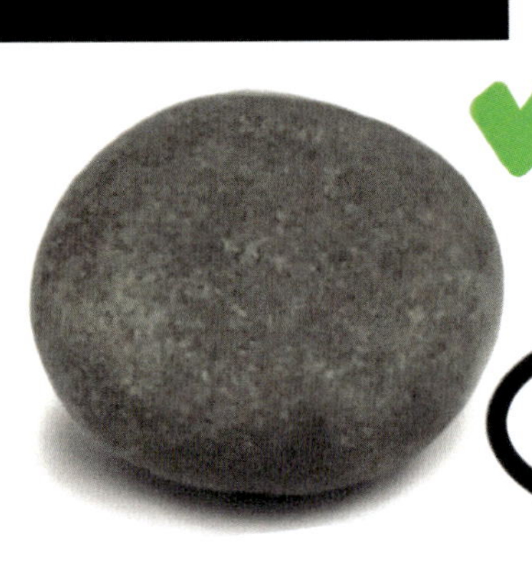

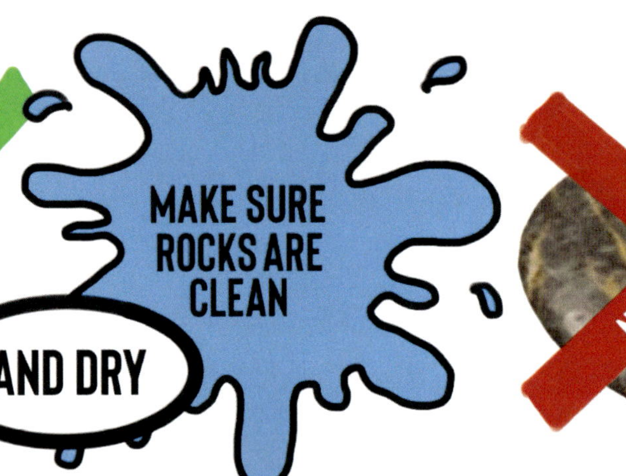

NO SHINY ROCKS

Paint

You can also use traditional acrylic paint!

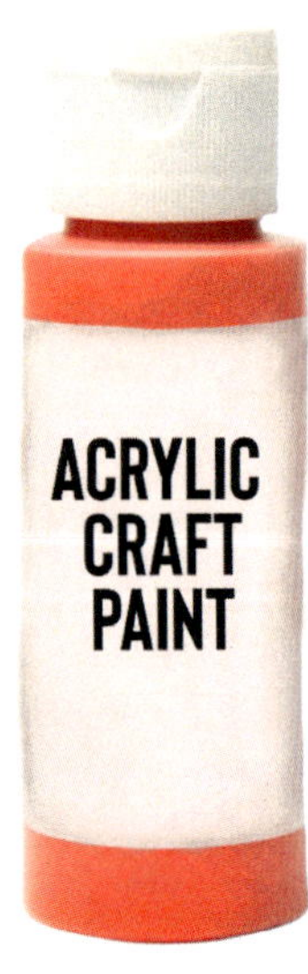

Acrylic craft paint is the best paint to use. It is very pigmented so it doesn't require as many layers.

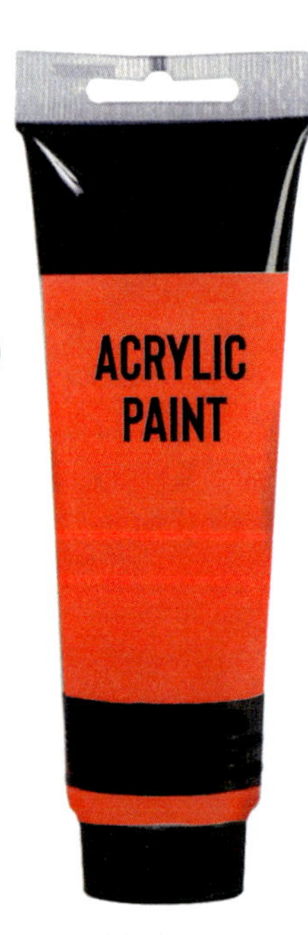

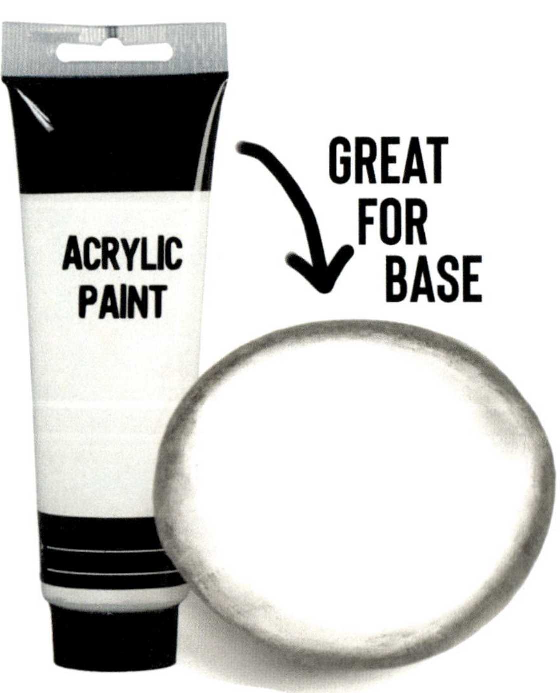

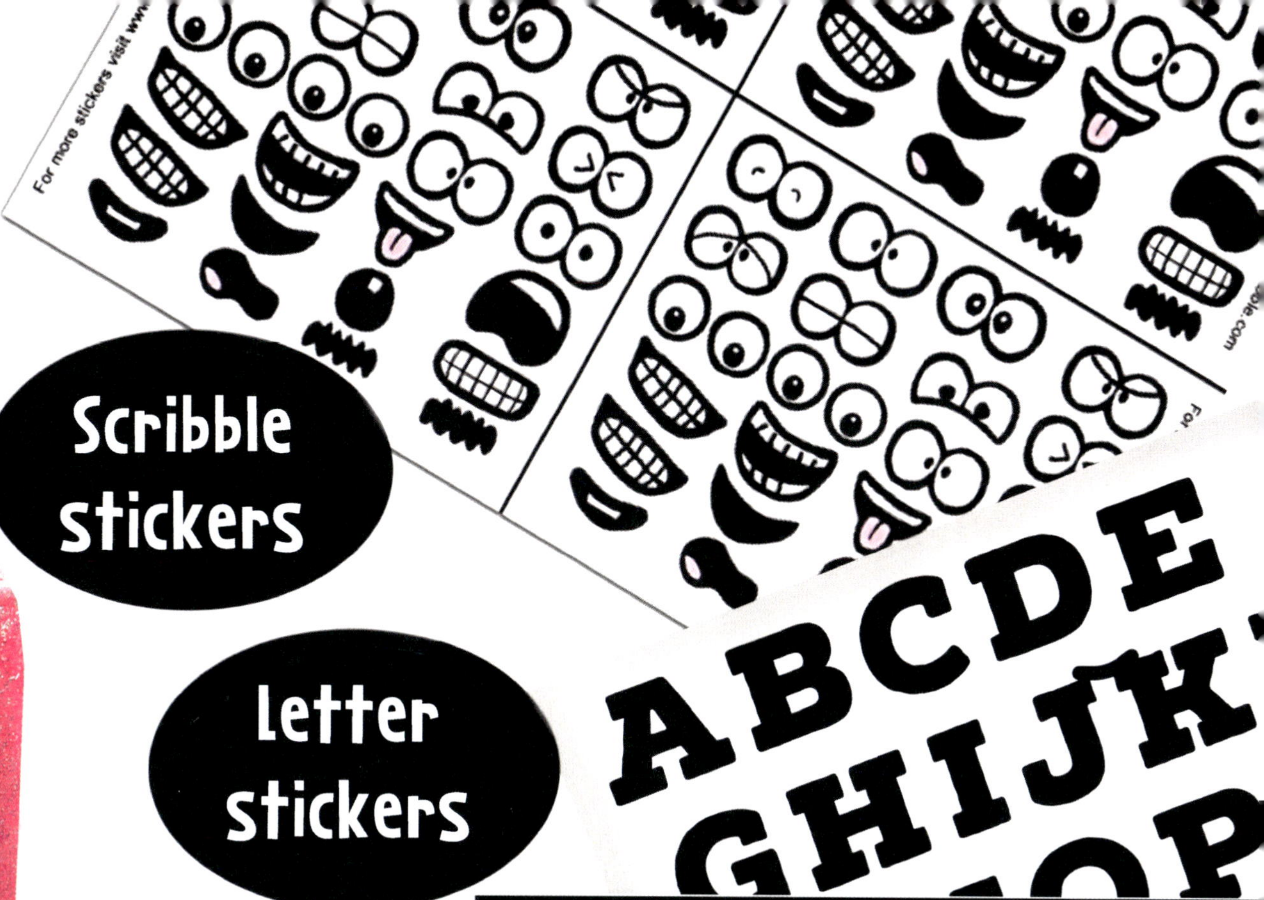

Scribble stickers

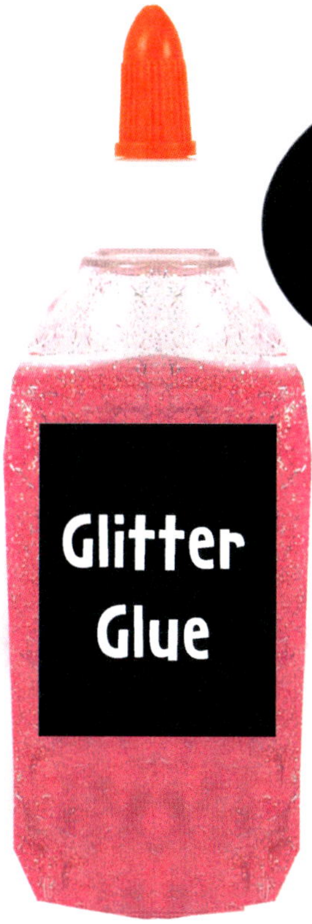

Letter stickers

Glitter Glue

Any stickers will work!

*Scribble stickers are available to purchase on www.dianealber.com

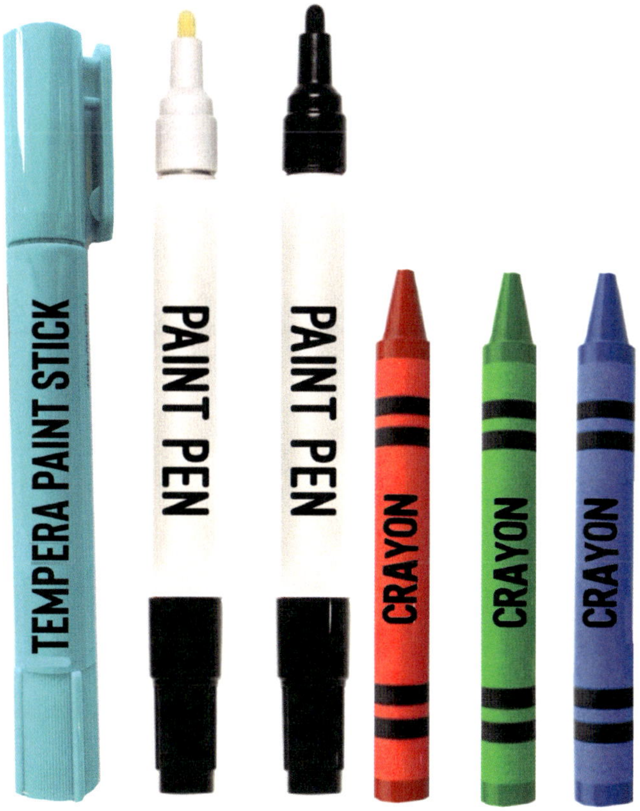

TEMPERA PAINT STICK

PAINT PEN

PAINT PEN

CRAYON

CRAYON

CRAYON

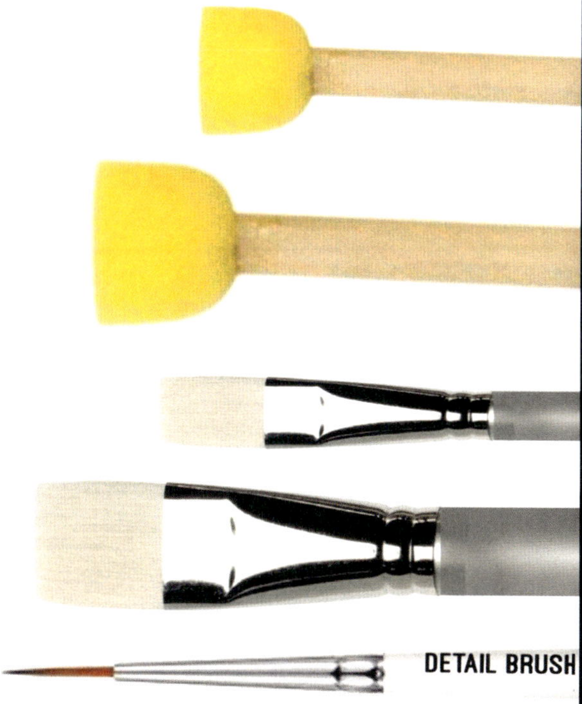

Brushes

DETAIL BRUSH

There are colors beyond what is shown here.

*PAINT PENS SHOULD ALWAYS BE USED WITH ADULT SUPERVISION

I wanted to create a book that could grow with the artist.

Here's the idea: A beginner might complete Steps 1-4, while someone with more experience could continue all the way through Step 7!

Take this example of a lime slice:

Steps 1-4 would be for a beginner (Ages 4-6)

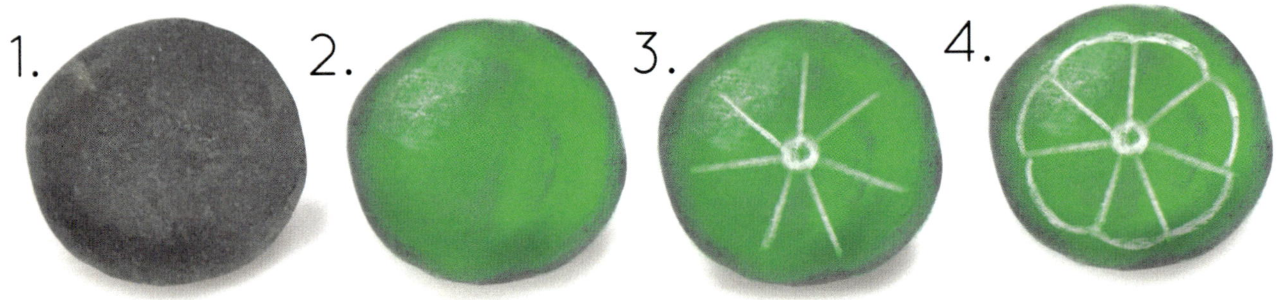

More advanced (Ages 7-10) could continue to Step 7

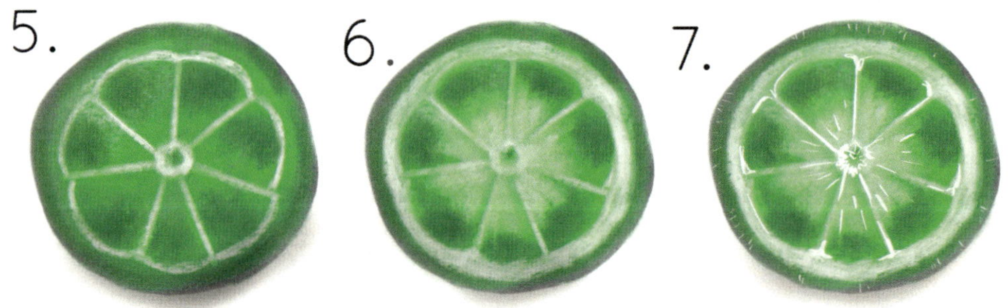

Beginner Tips

Ages (4-6)

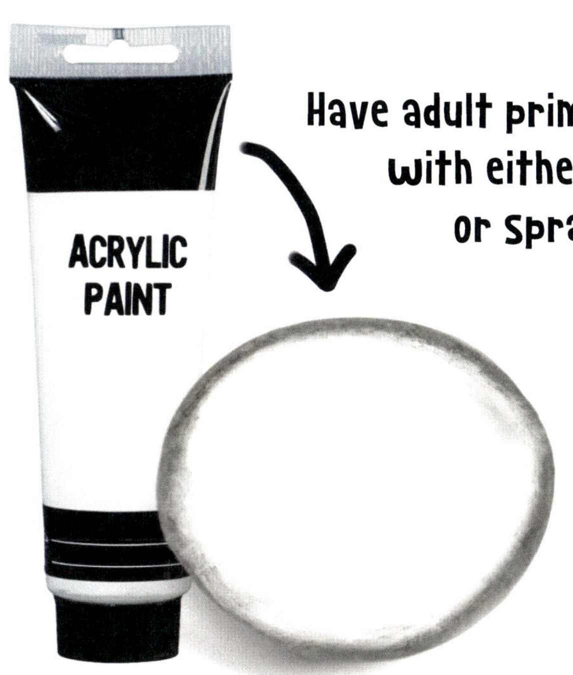

Have adult prime the rock first
with either tube paint
or spray paint!

Glitter Glue
is great for
adding some
sparkle!

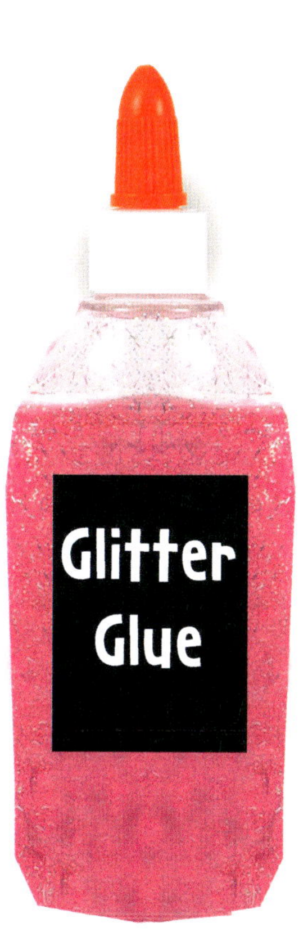

Best Material to use (Ages 4-6)

*Tempera Paint Sticks are easy to control with little mess, and they are non-toxic and washable!

*Dark colored crayons work best on a white base rock to provide the most contrast!

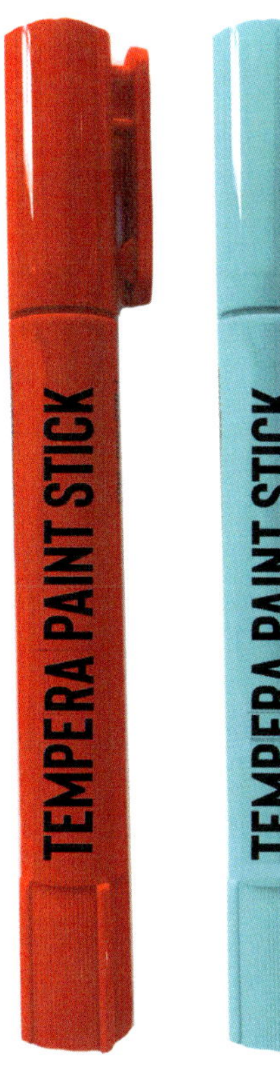

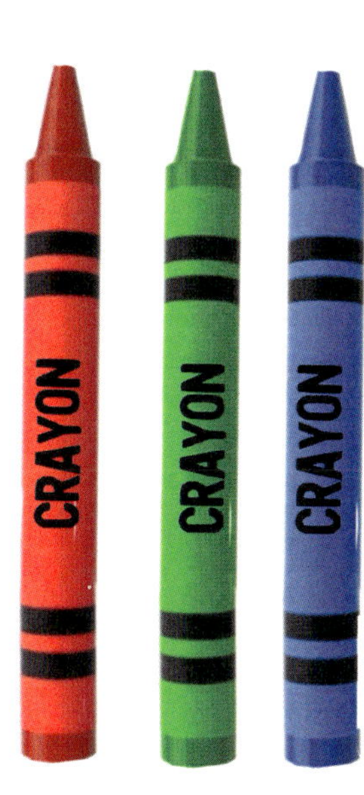

Masking

is the art of protecting an area from change. For example, the use of stickers or masking tape would prevent that area of the stone from being colored.

PAINT OR TEMPERA PAINT STICKS WORK GREAT!

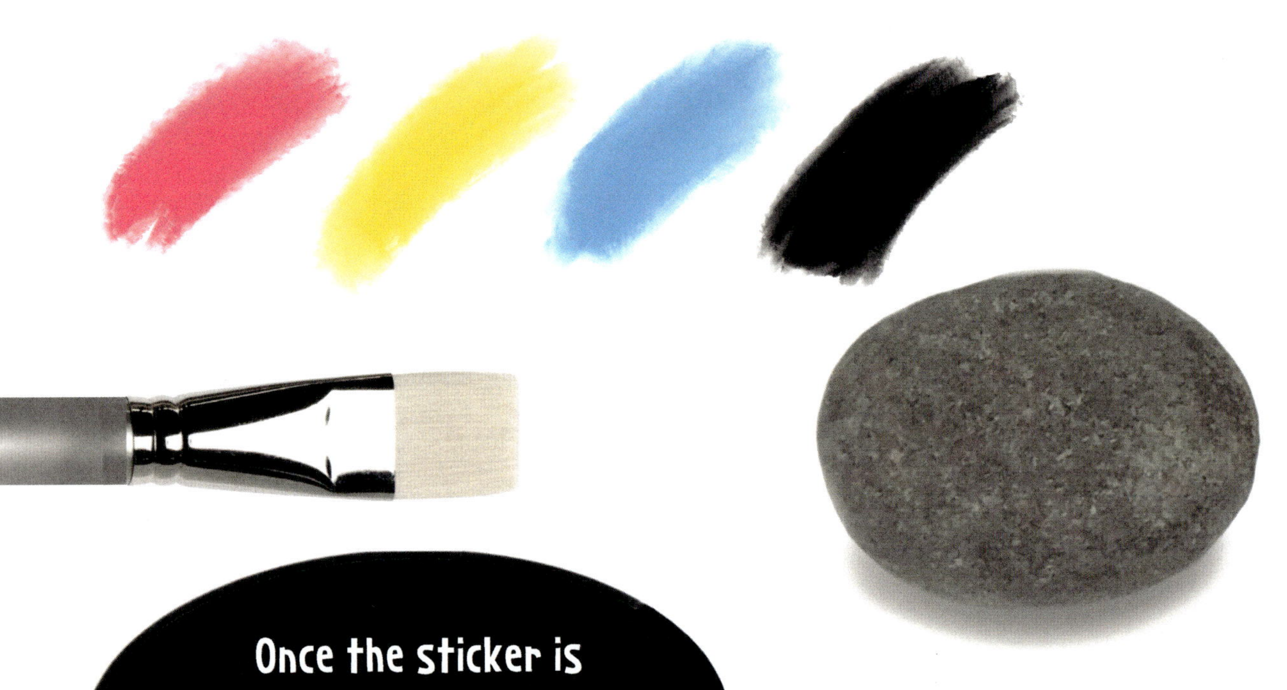

Once the sticker is peeled off the background color remains.

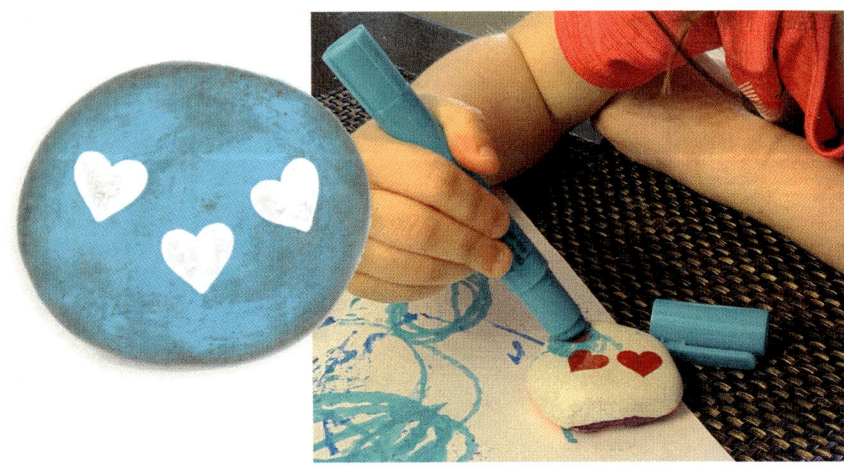

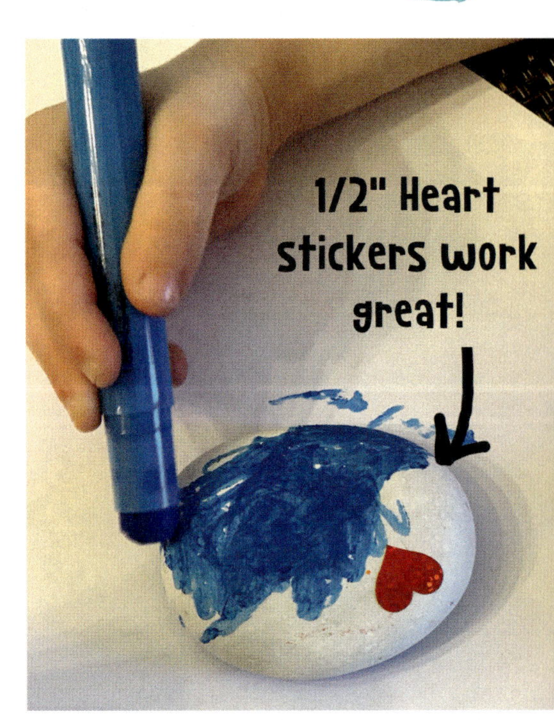

1/2" Heart stickers work great!

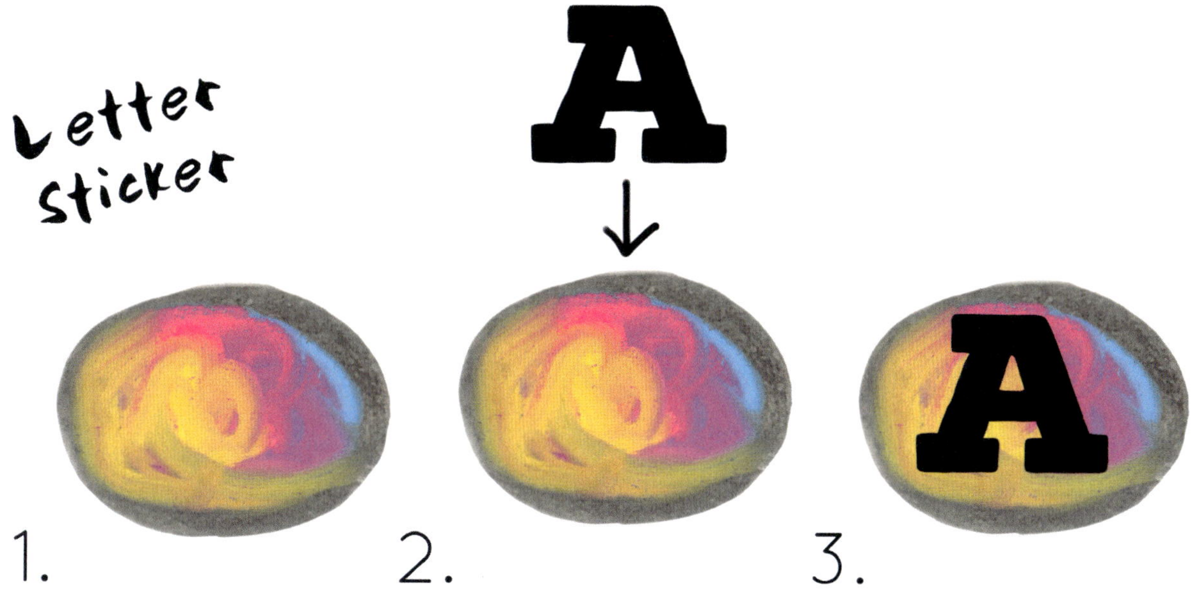

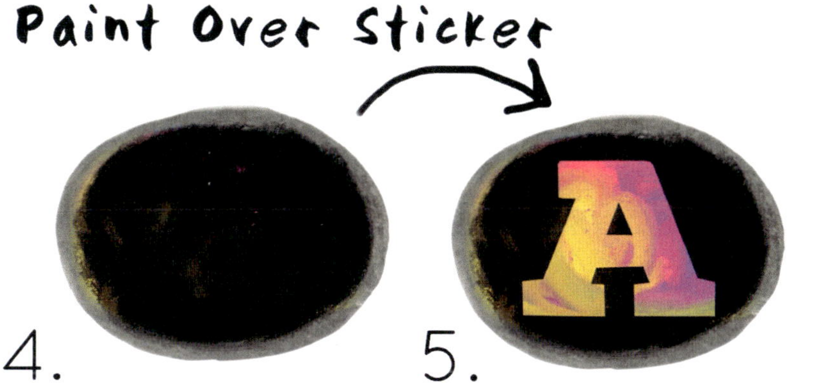

Letter Sticker

A

1.

2.

3.

Paint Over Sticker

4.

5.

Peel Sticker Off

TIP: Make sure you peel off the sticker when the paint is still WET!

OTHER VARIATIONS

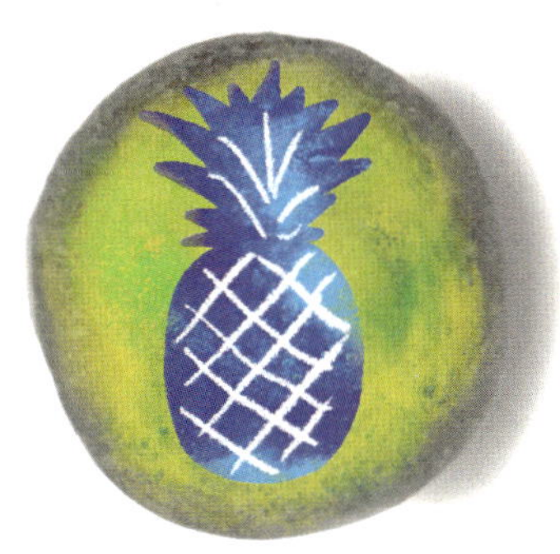

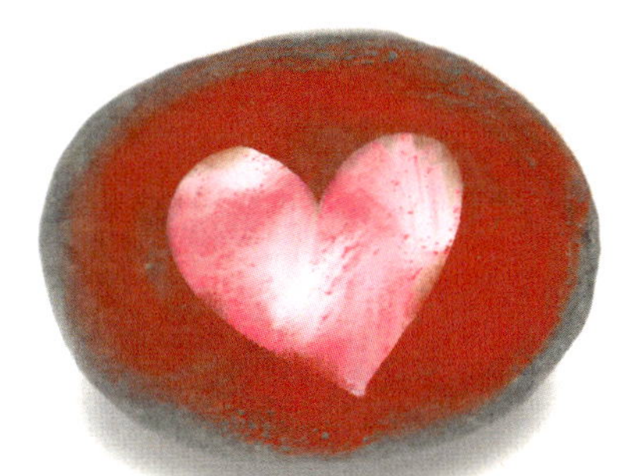

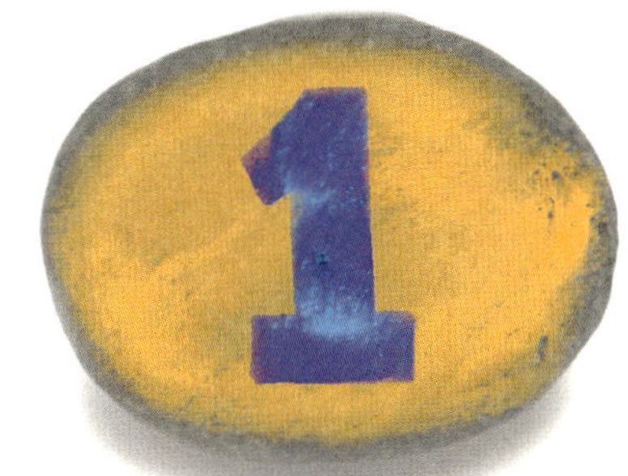

Letters and Lines

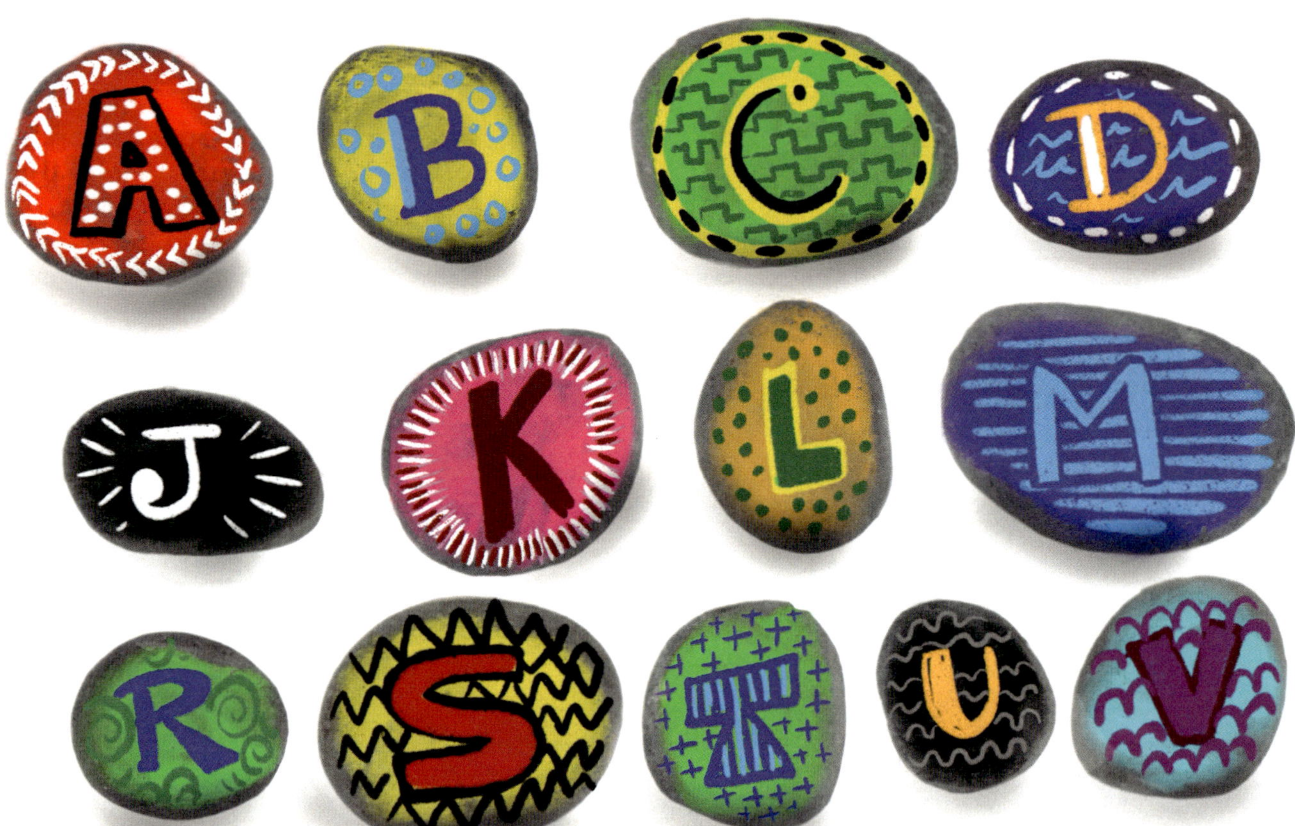

DOTTED

BOUNCE

DASH

STARS

THICK & THIN

CHEVRON

CASTLE

CURVE

CROSSHATCH

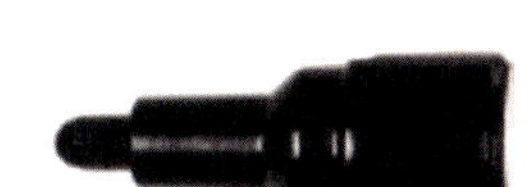

DETAIL BRUSH

PAINT PEN

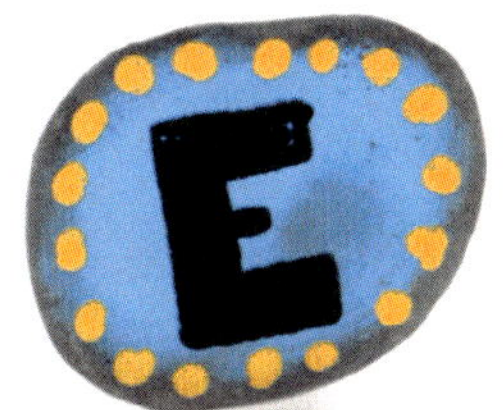

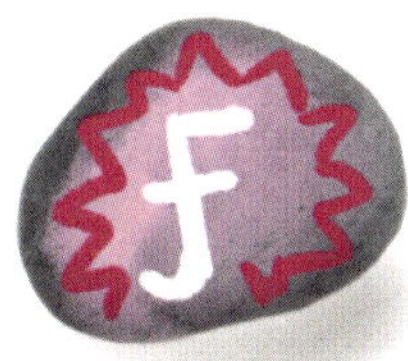

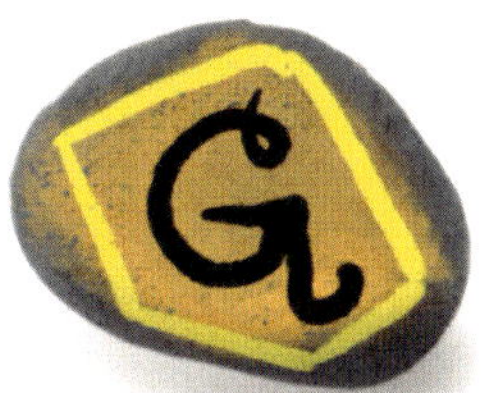

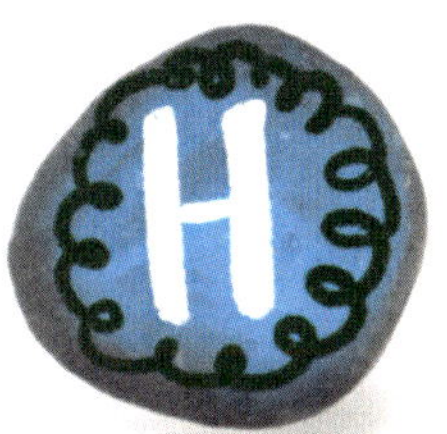

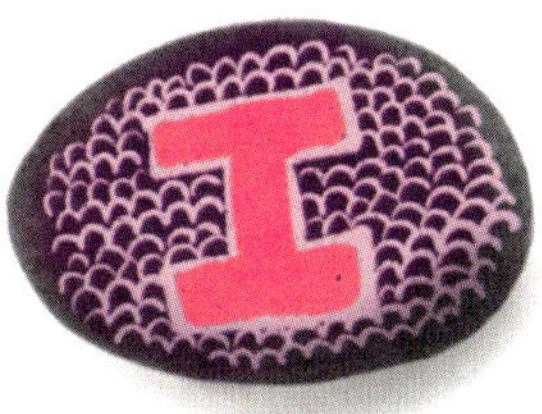

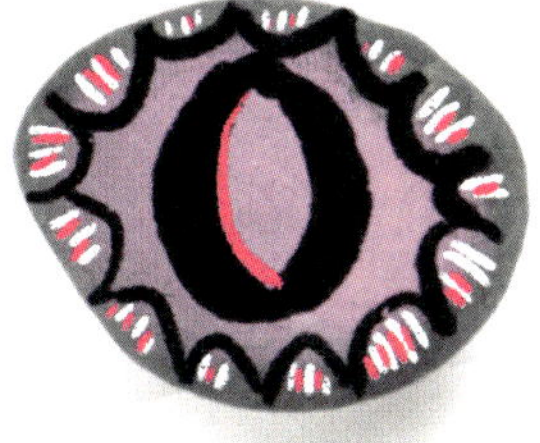

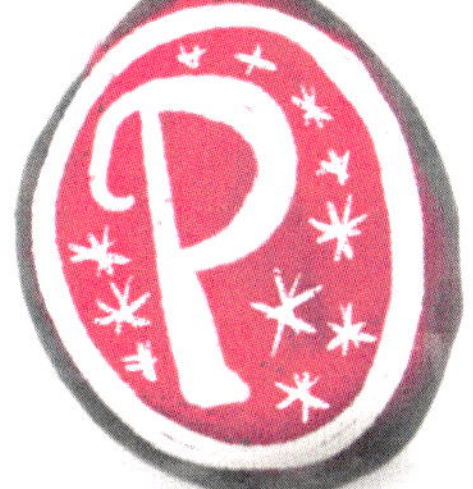

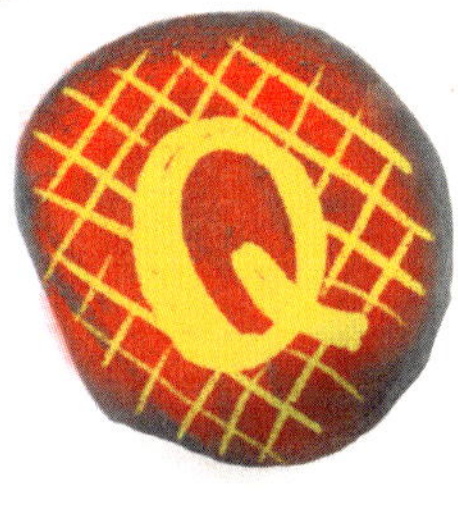

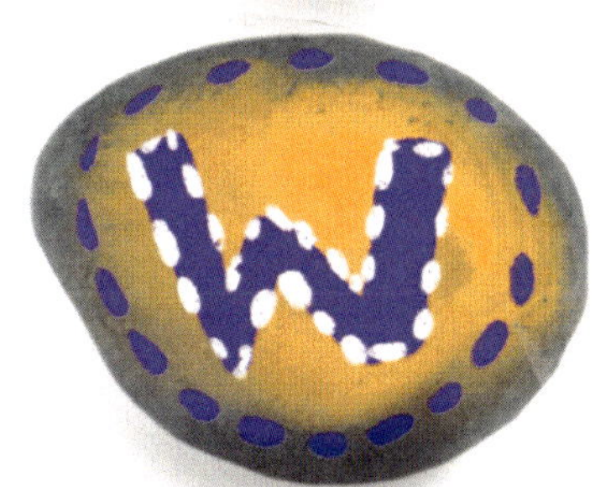

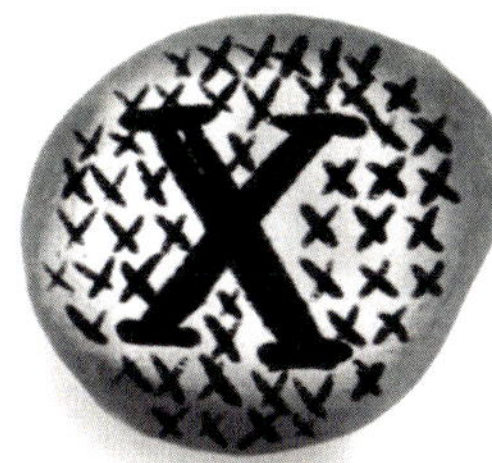

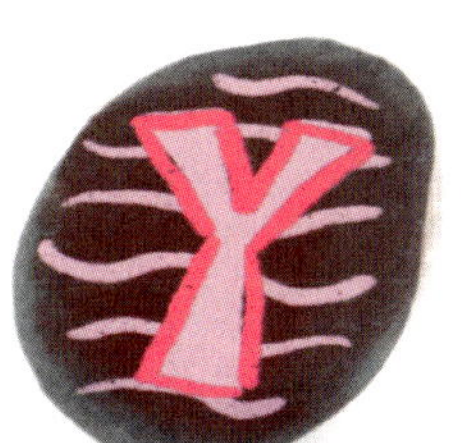

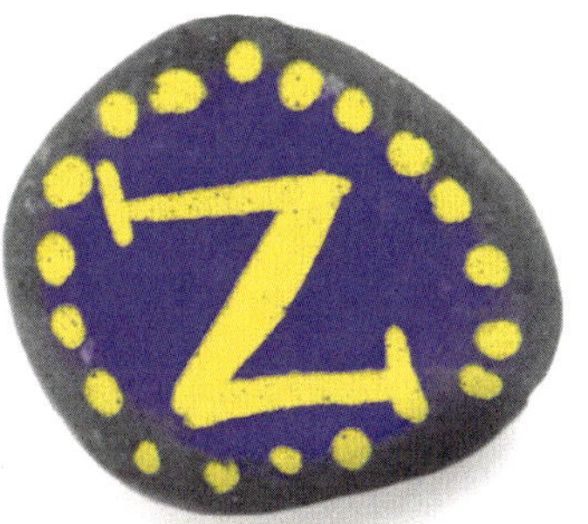

ZIGZAG

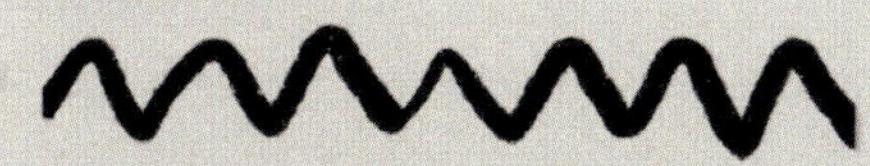

CRISS CROSS

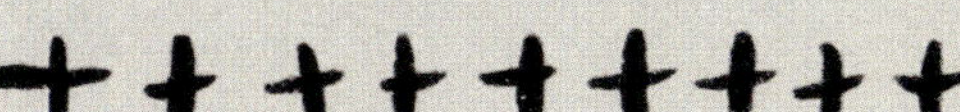

SPIRAL

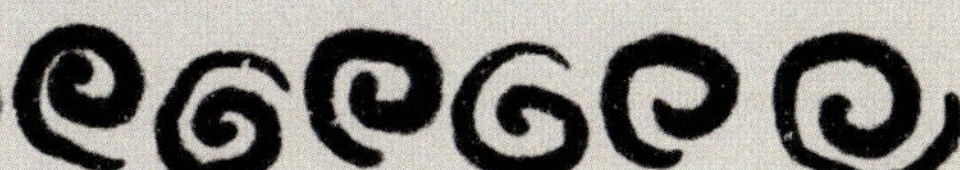

CURLY

OCEAN WAVE

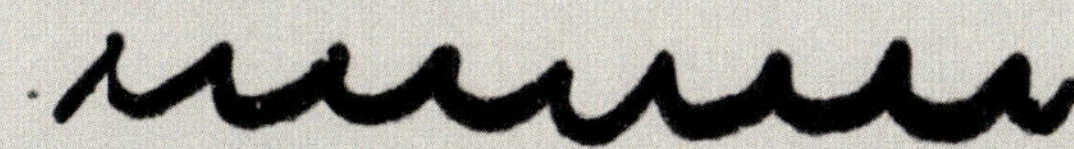

DIAGONAL

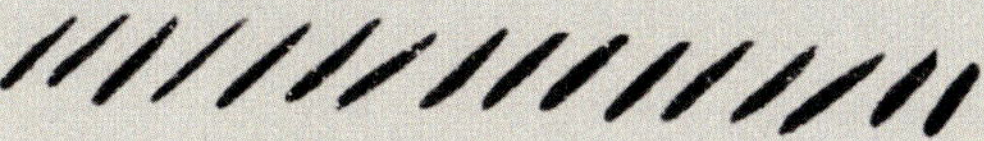

VERTICAL & HORIZONTAL

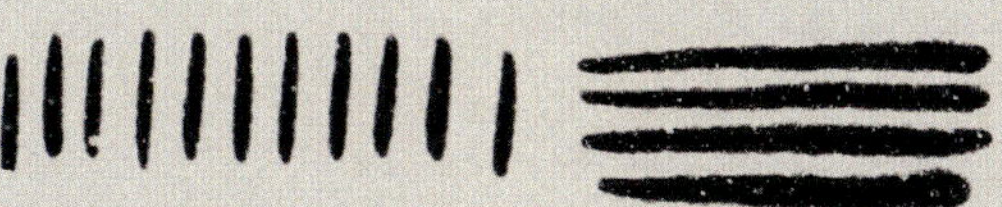

WAVY

Easy Scribble Stone

Great for ages 2-4

Adults should always paint the base to make it easier for the child to scribble. You can either use white acrylic paint or a primer spray paint.

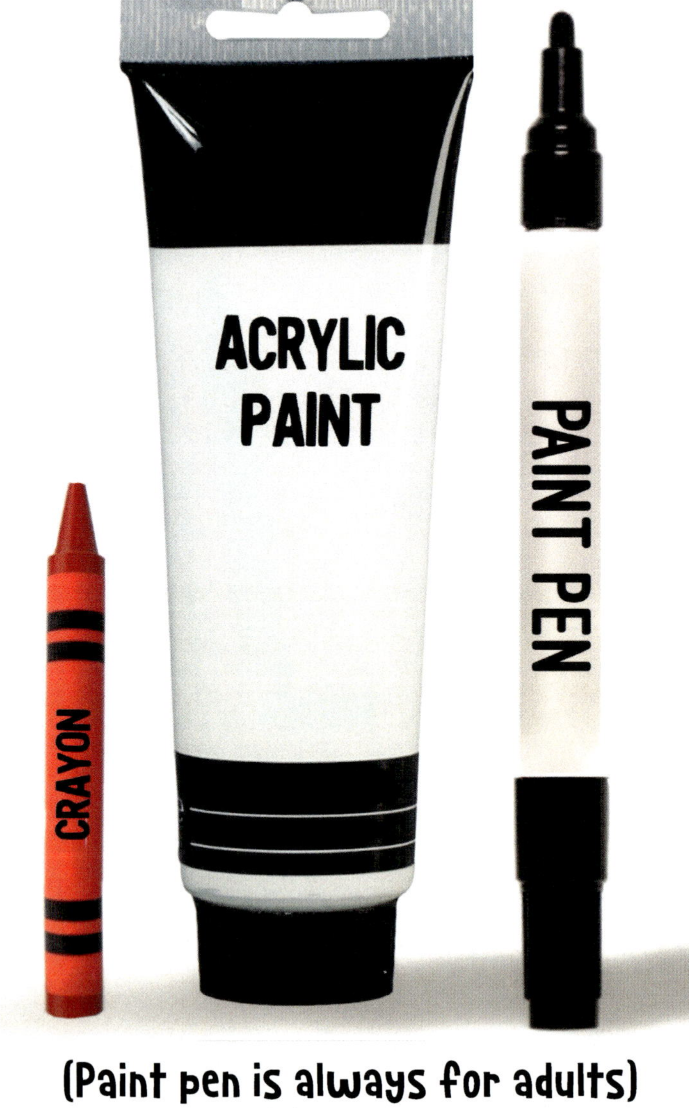

(Paint pen is always for adults)

Scribble stickers

STEP 1. Start with a white base.

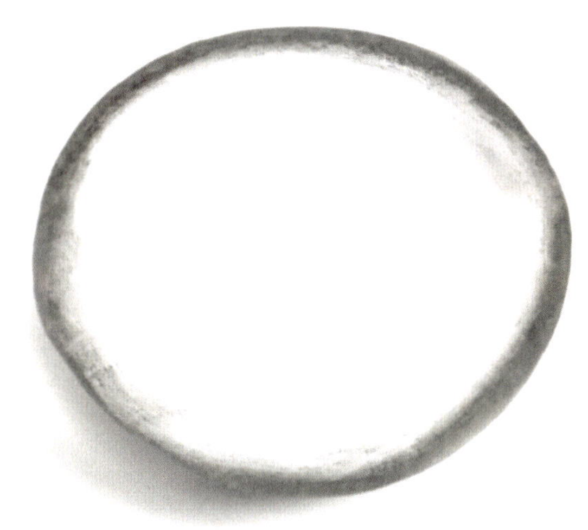

STEP 2.

Scribble with crayon.

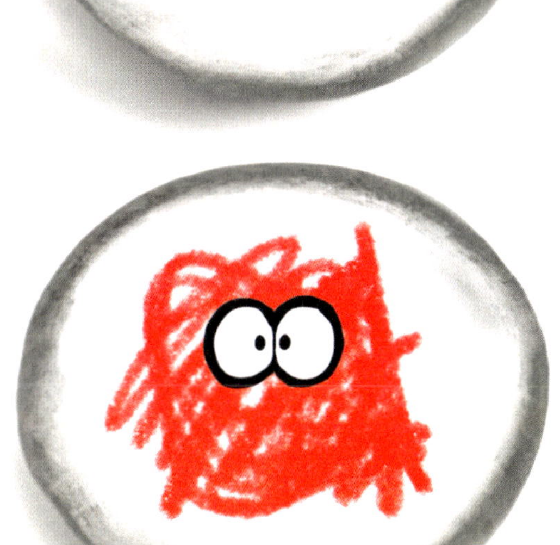

STEP 3.

Add Scribble stickers

STEP 4.

Add arms and legs with black paint pen or black crayon.

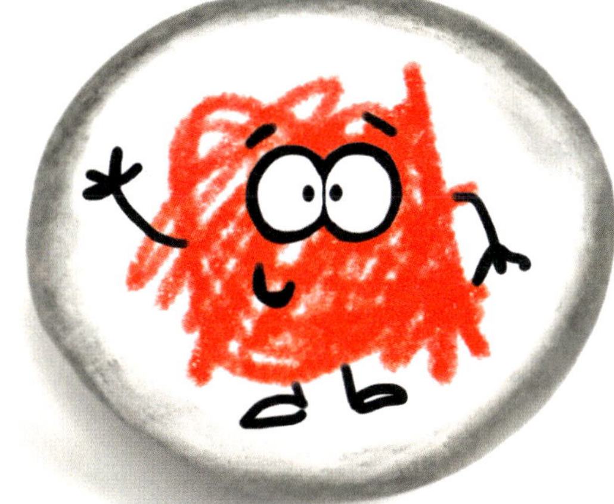

Spots

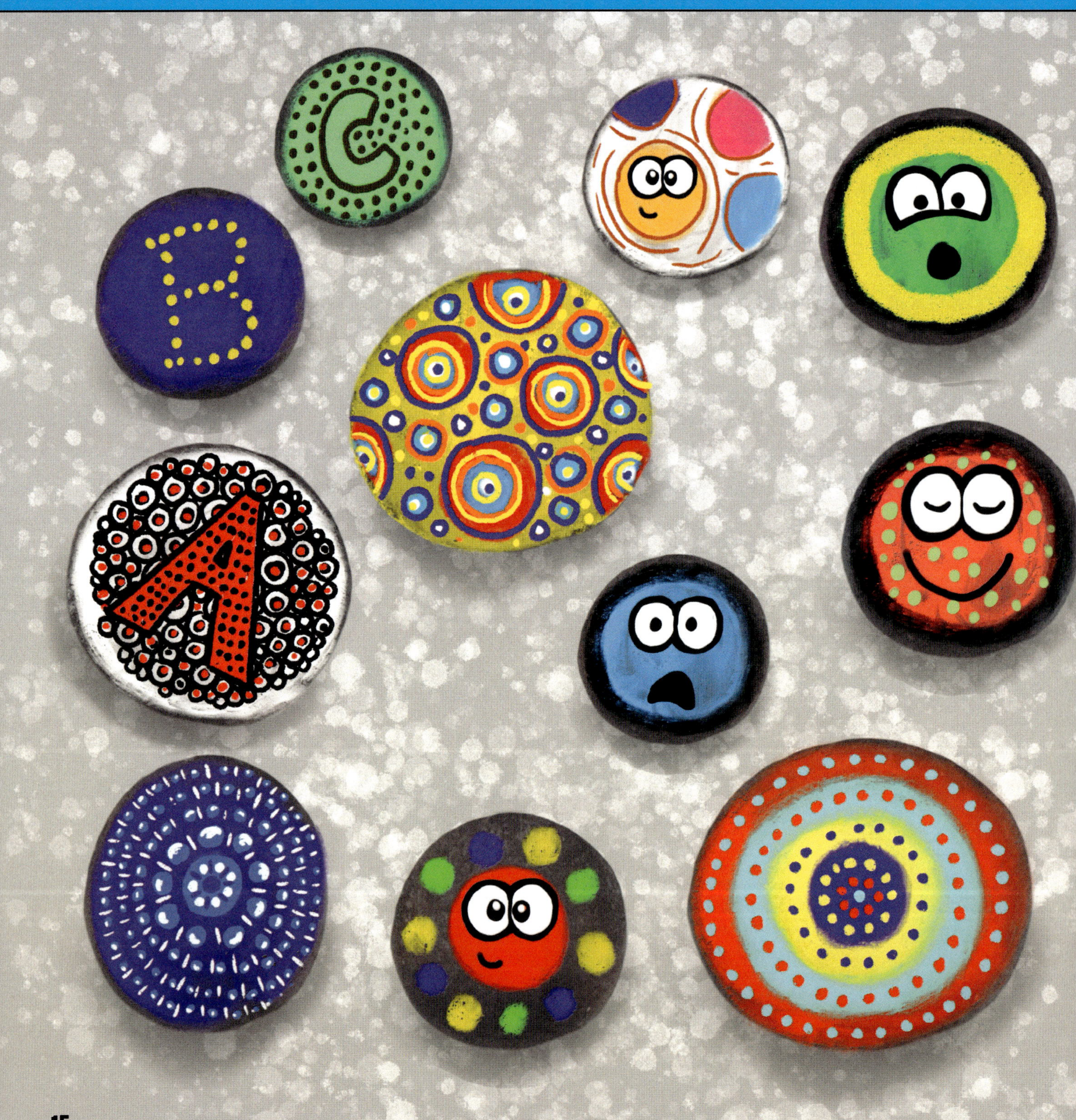

Make your own painting tools!

SMALL MARSHMALLOWS

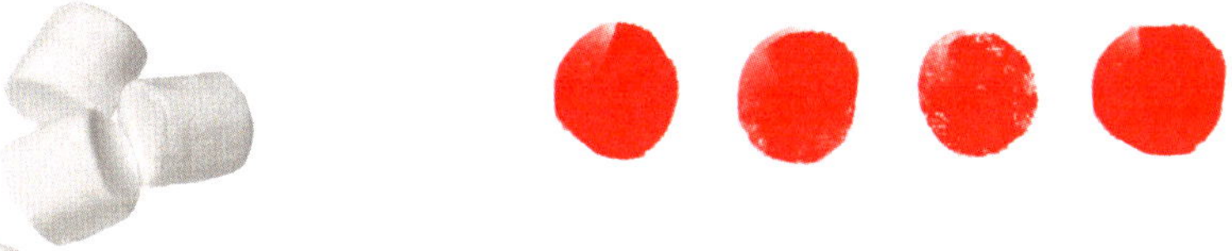

LARGE MARSHMALLOWS

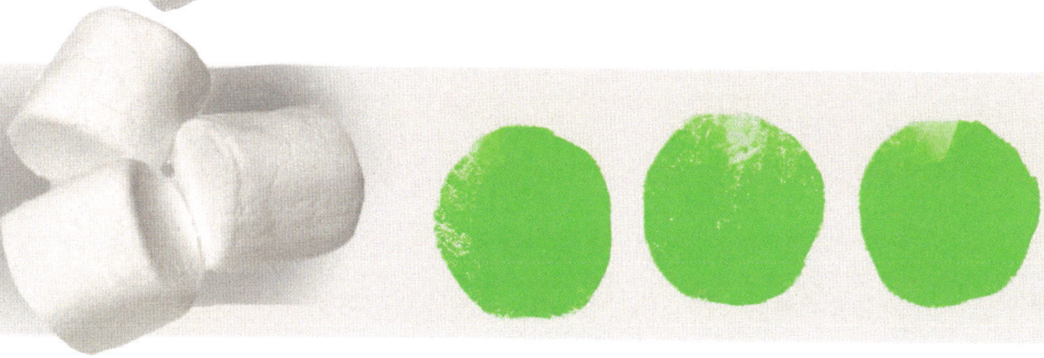

LARGE BUILDING BRICKS

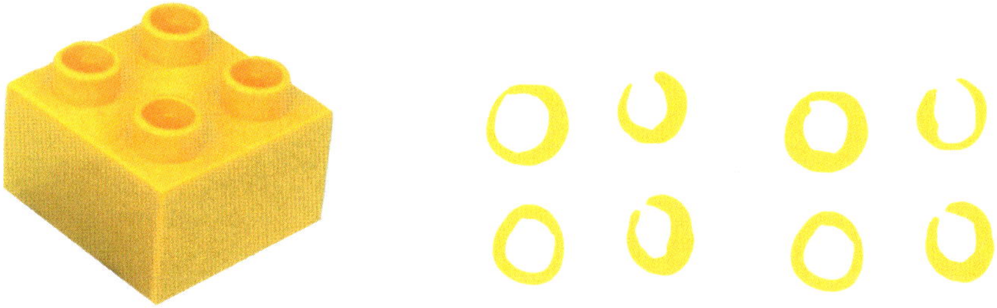

SMALL BUILDING BRICKS

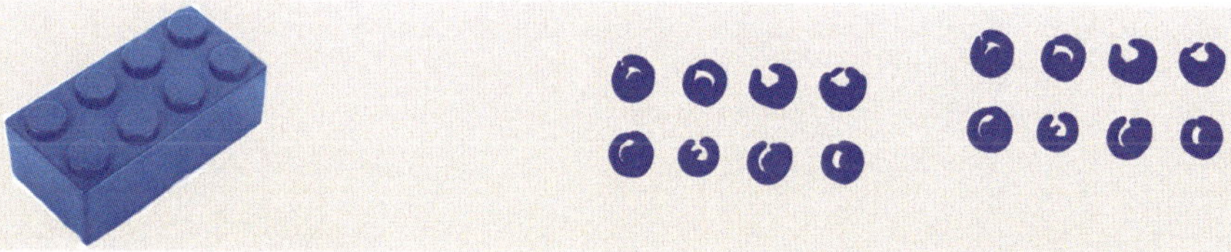

COTTON SWAB

BOBBY PIN

PENCIL ERASER

RIGATONI NOODLE

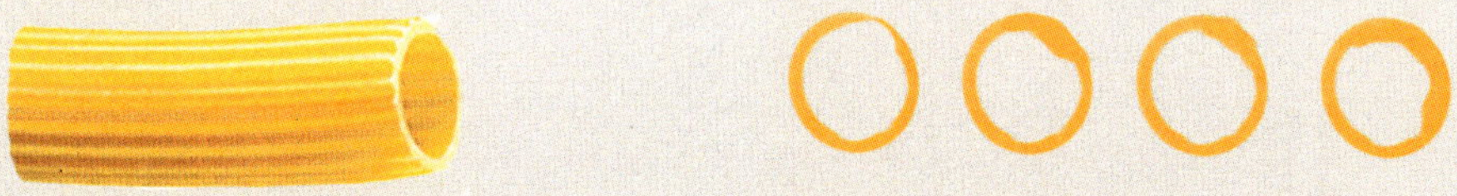

BUBBLE WRAP

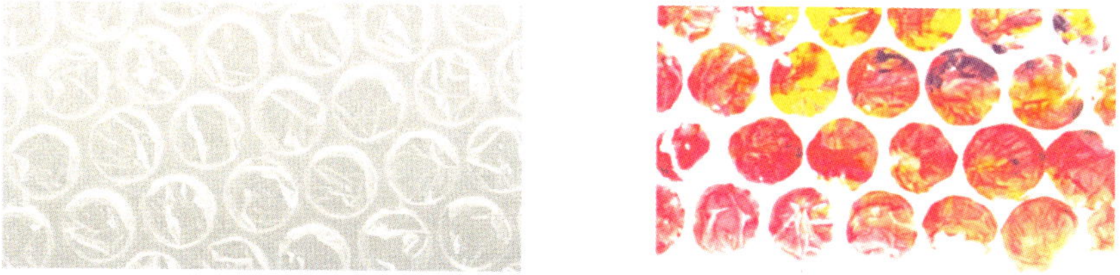

Triangles and Squares

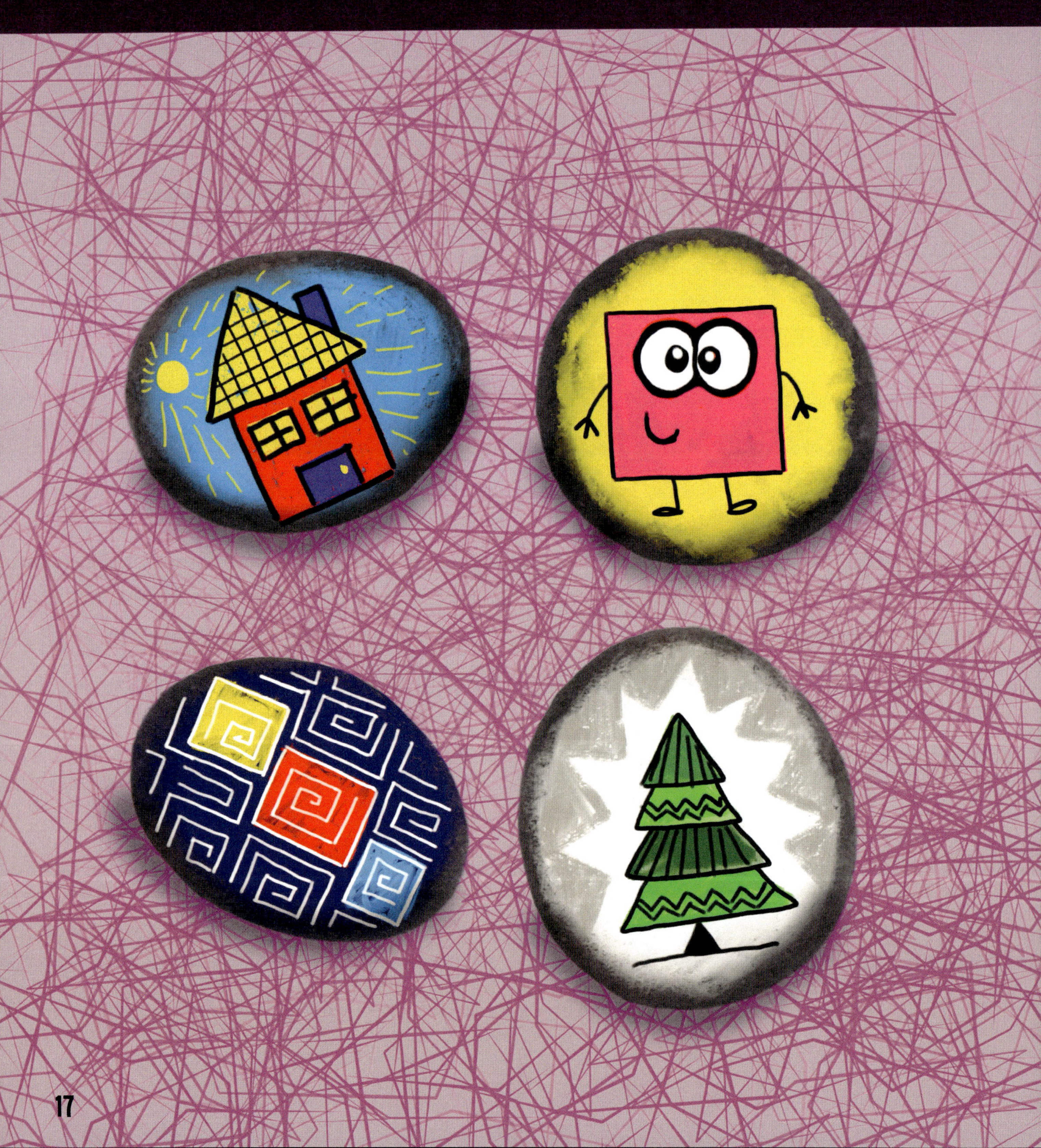

YOU WILL NEED:

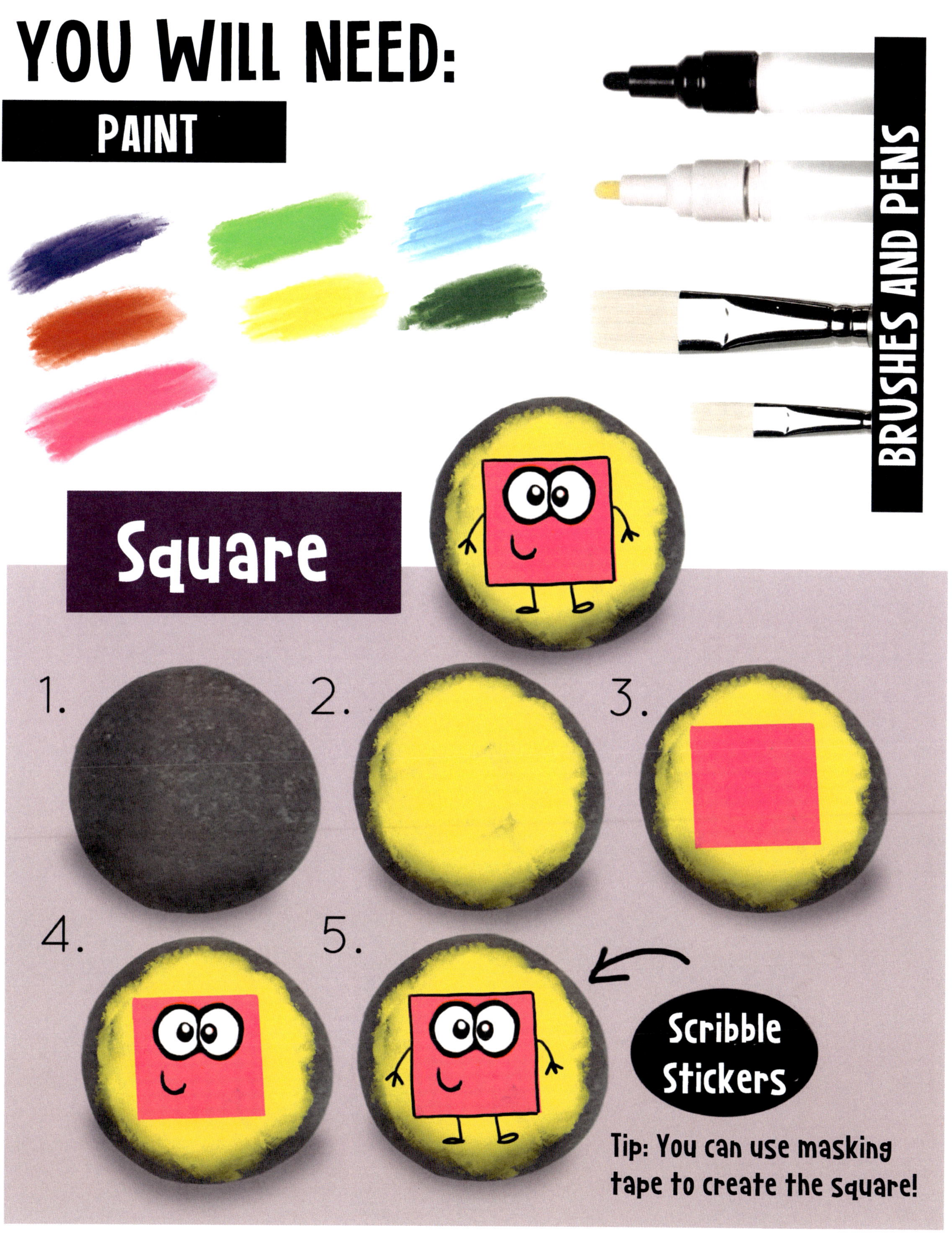

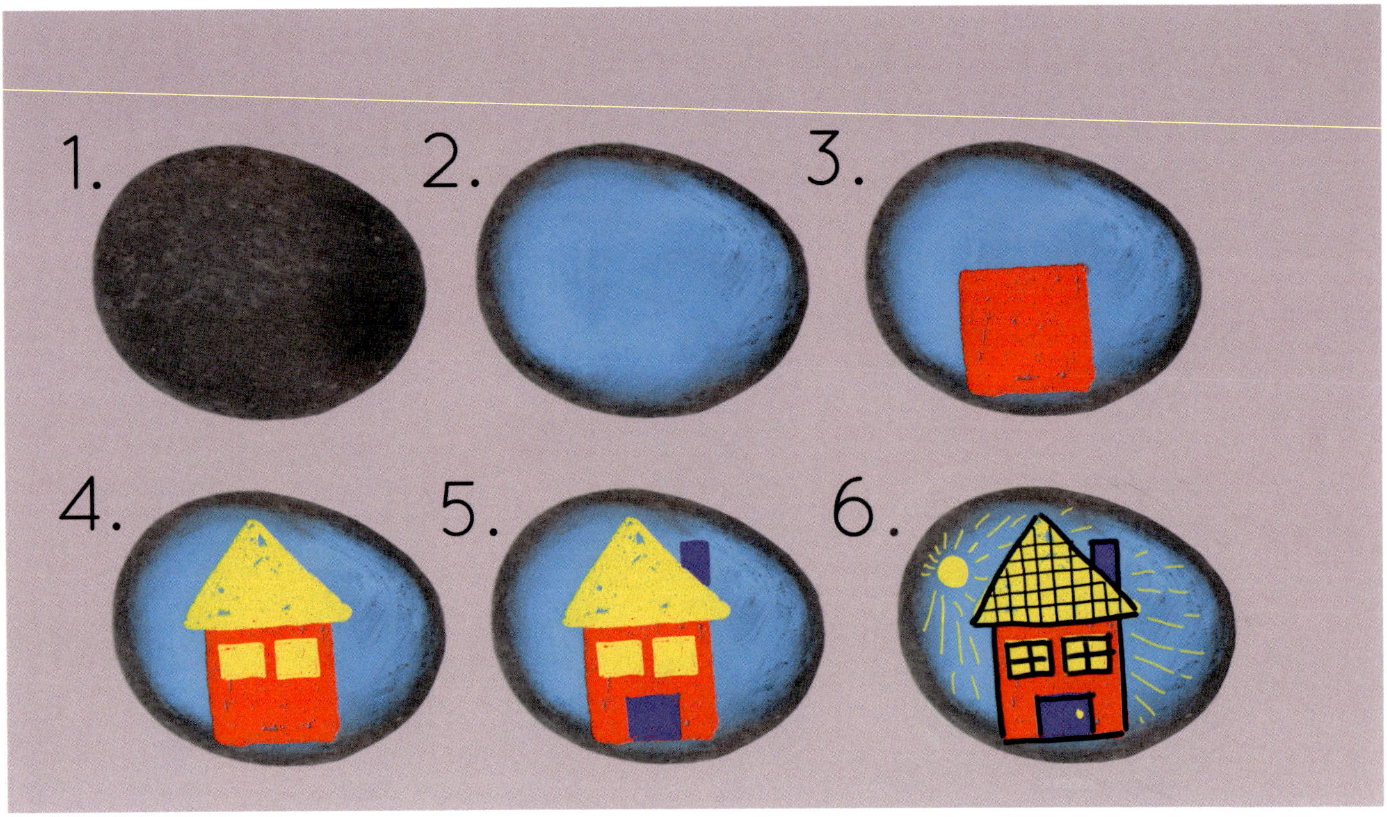

1. 2. 3.

4. 5. 6.

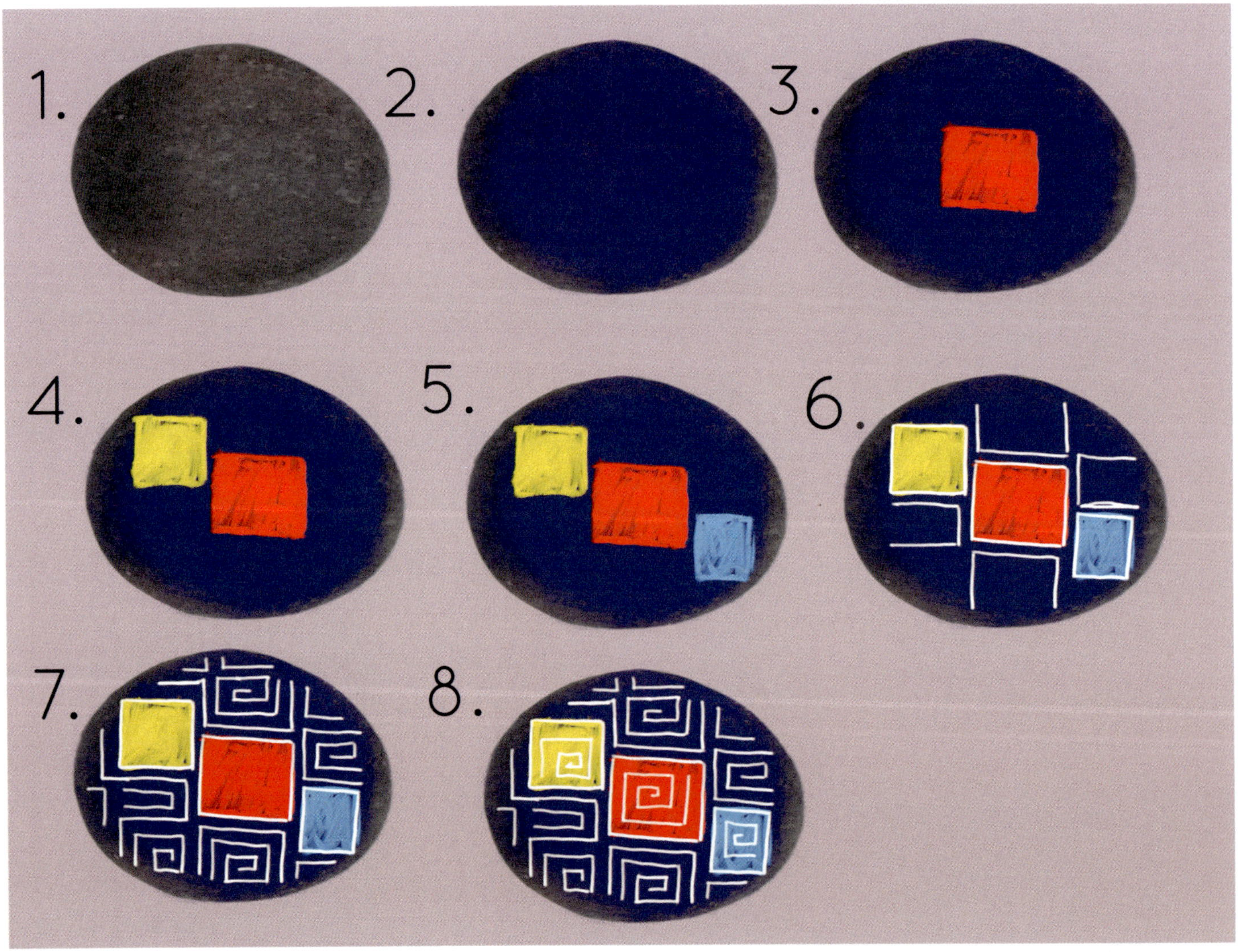

1. 2. 3.

4. 5. 6.

7. 8.

Triangle Tree

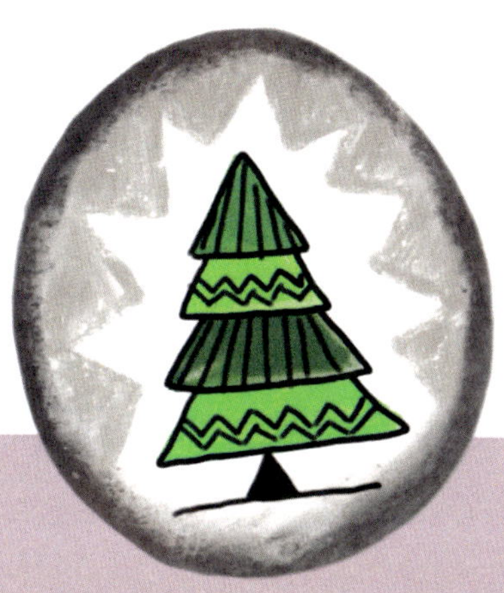

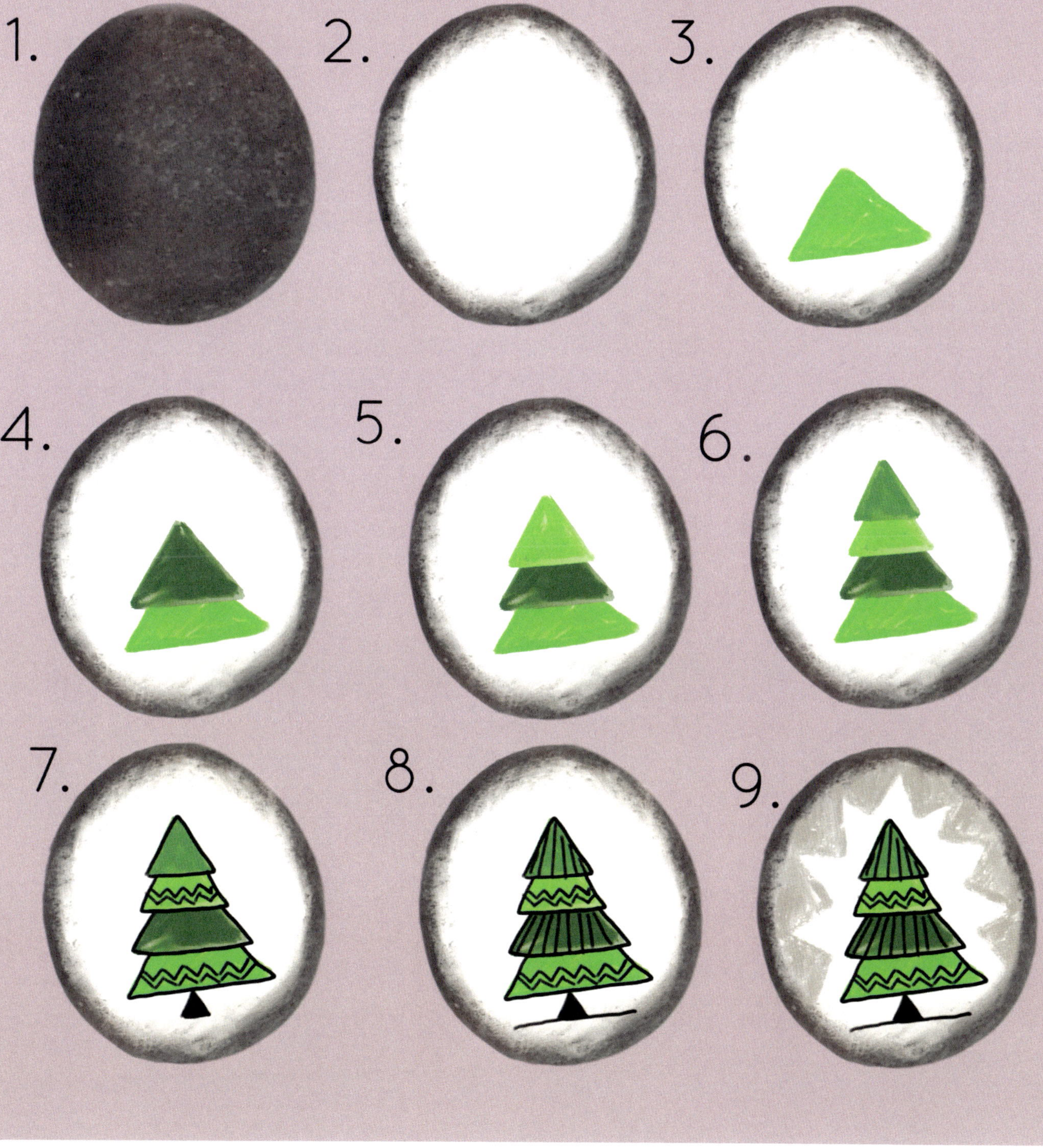

1.

2.

3.

4.

5.

6.

7.

8.

9.

Stars

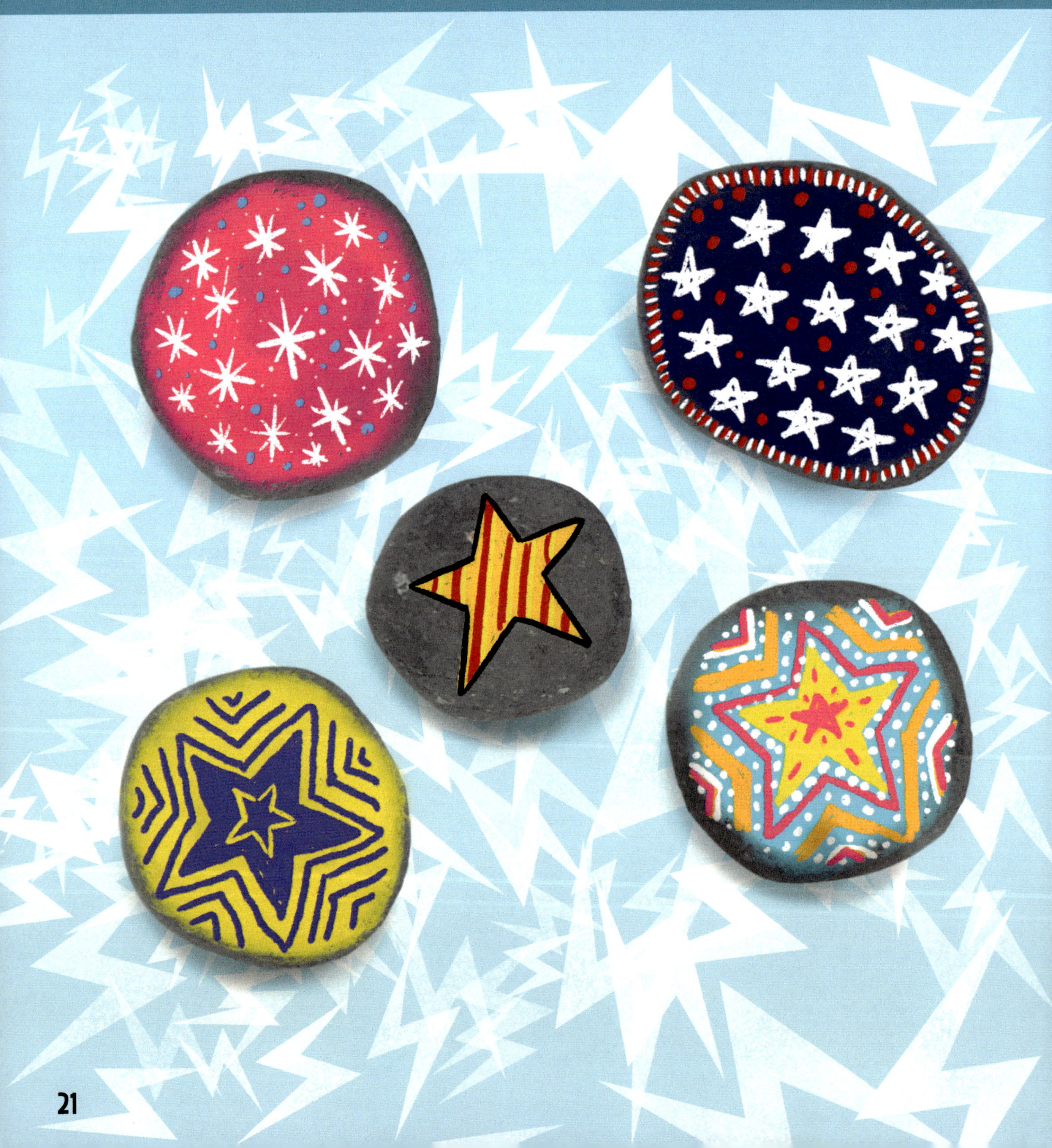

YOU WILL NEED:

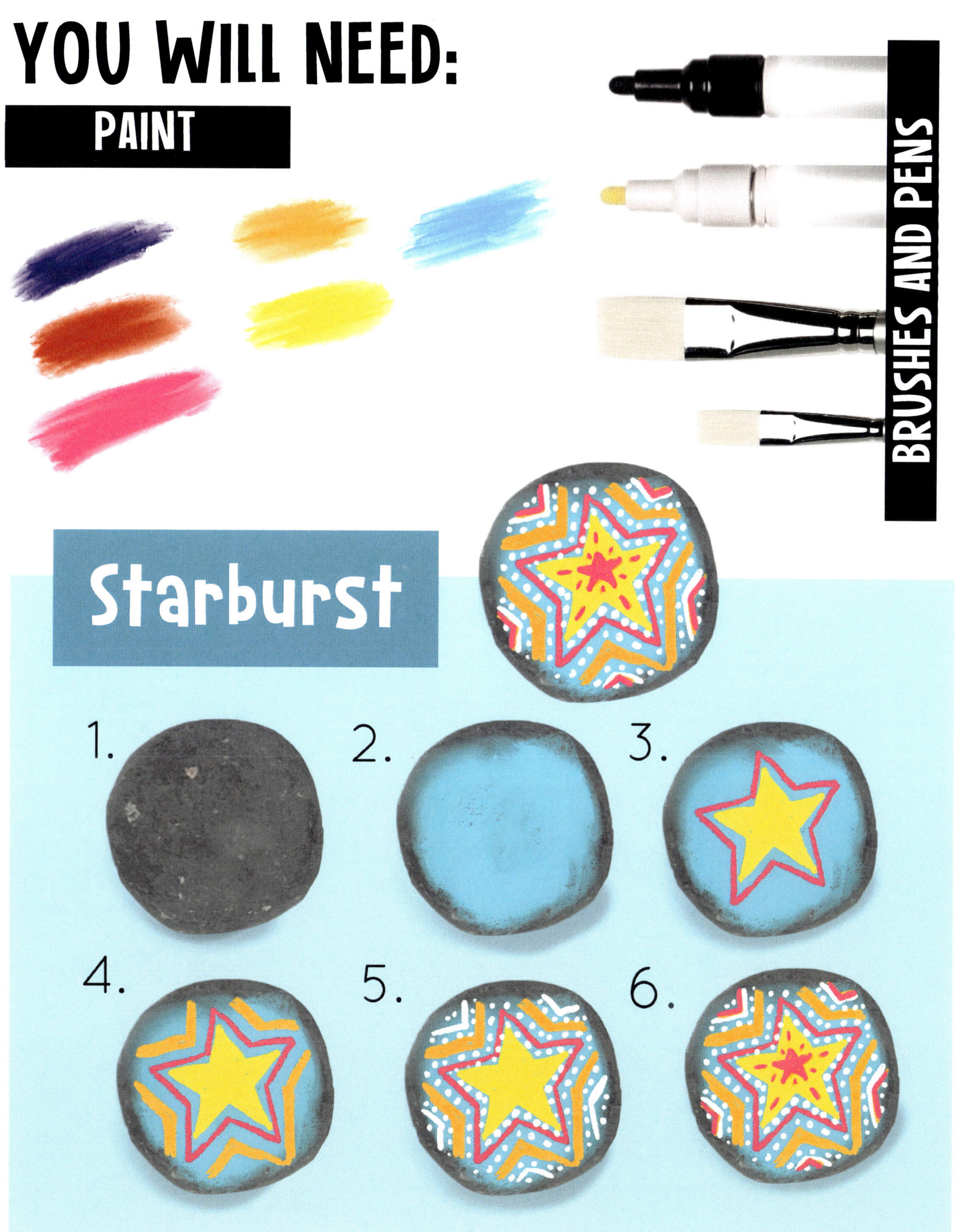

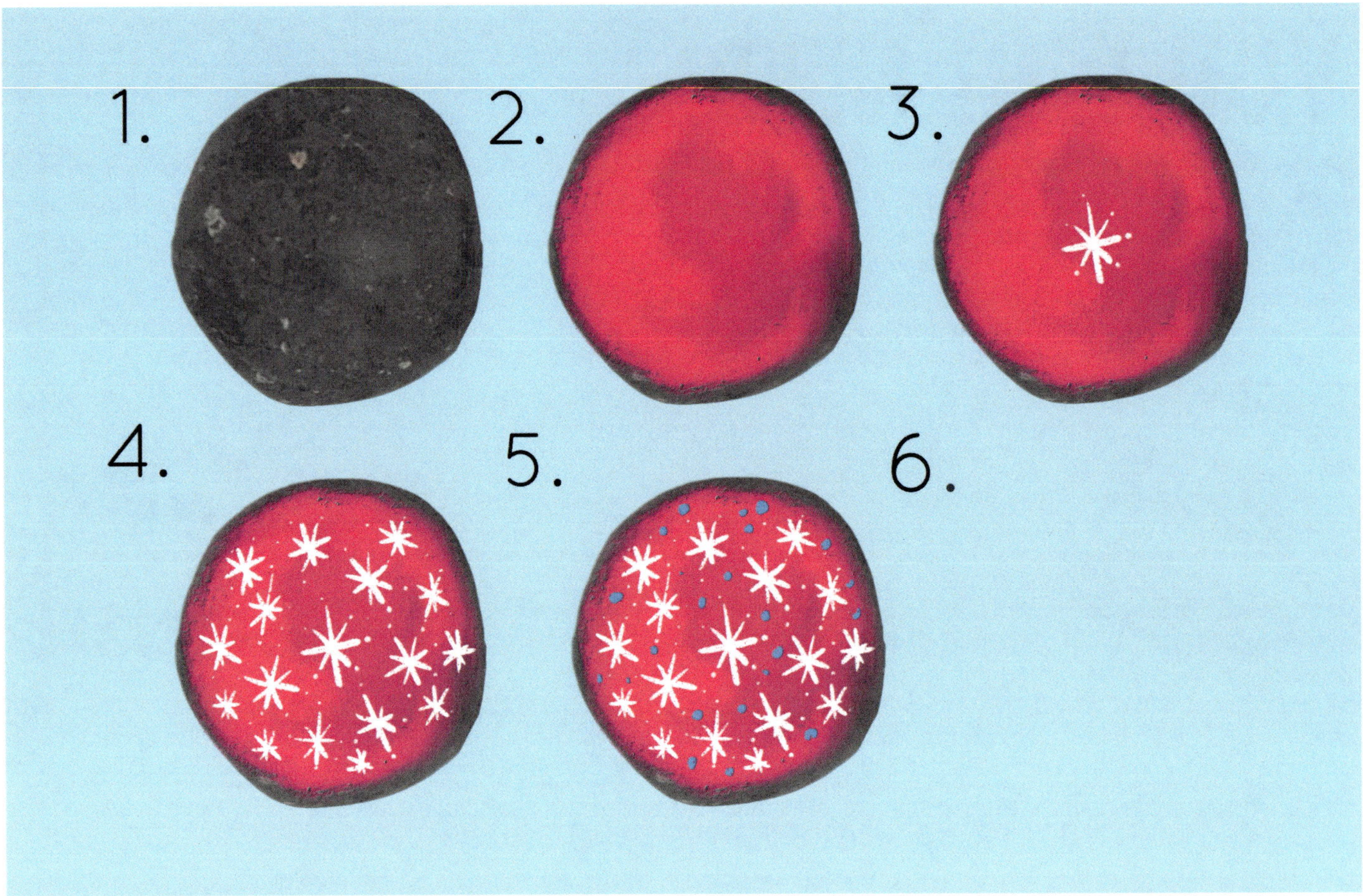

1. 2. 3.

4. 5. 6.

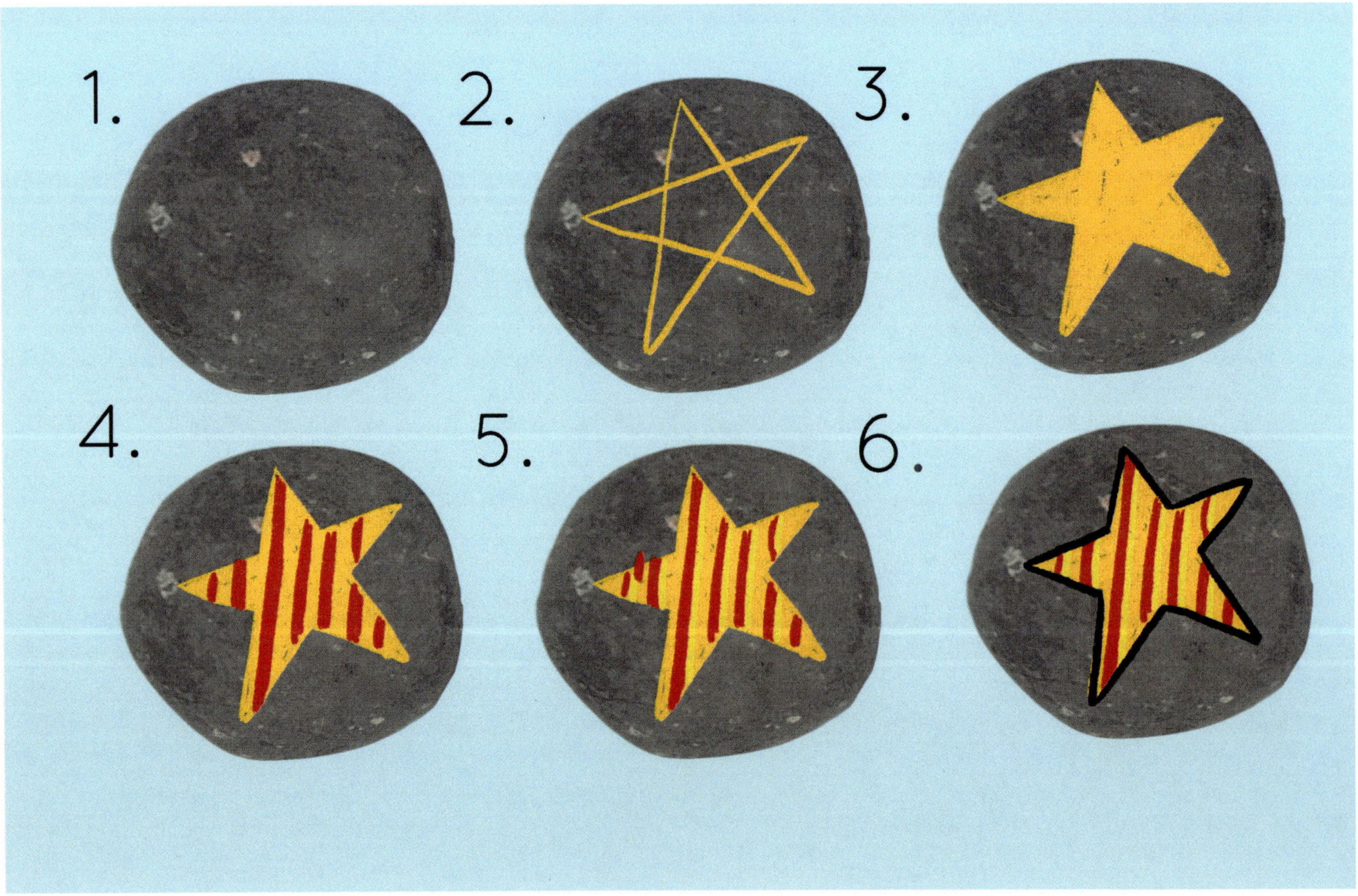

1. 2. 3.

4. 5. 6.

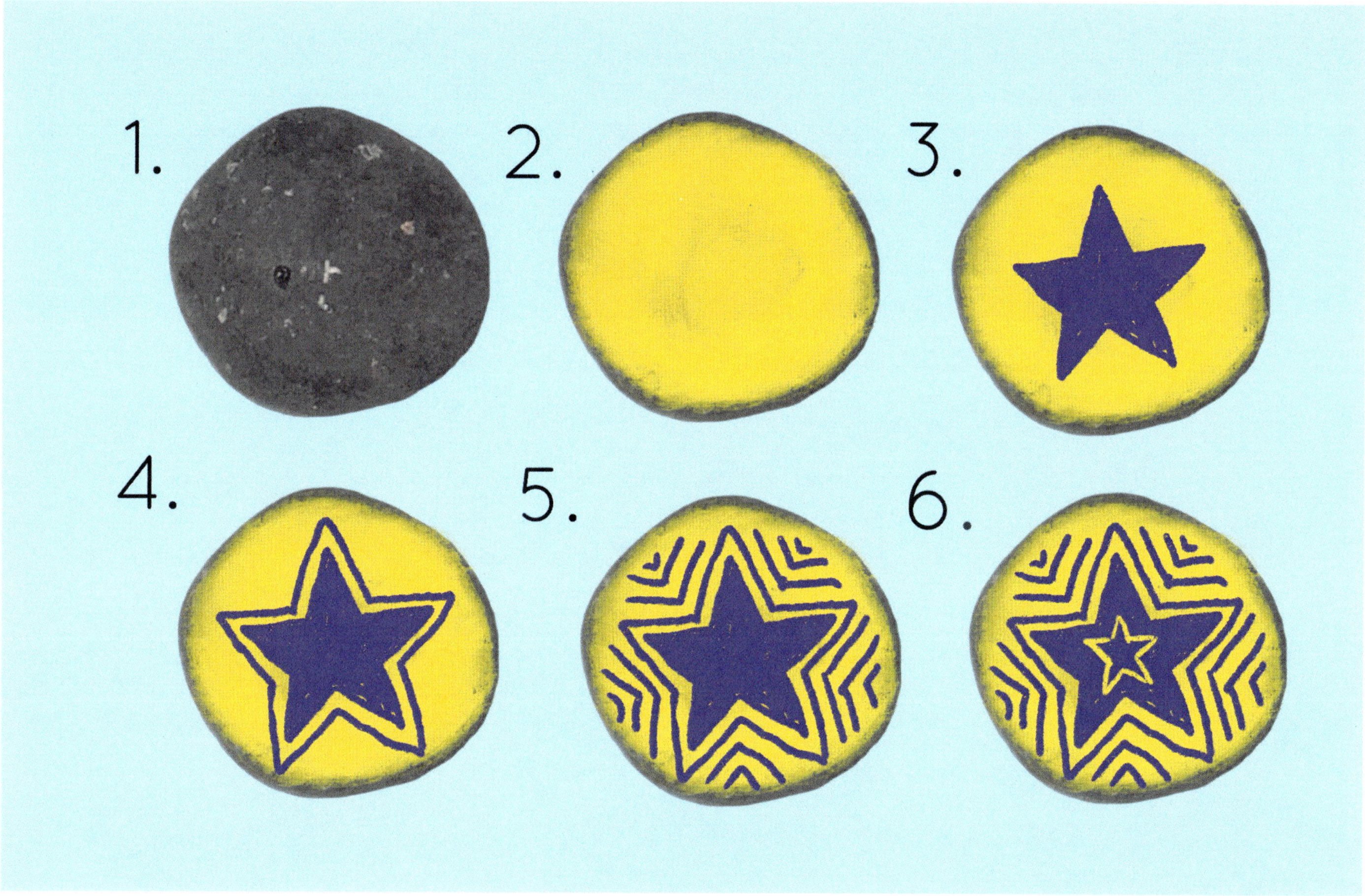

1. 2. 3.

4. 5. 6.

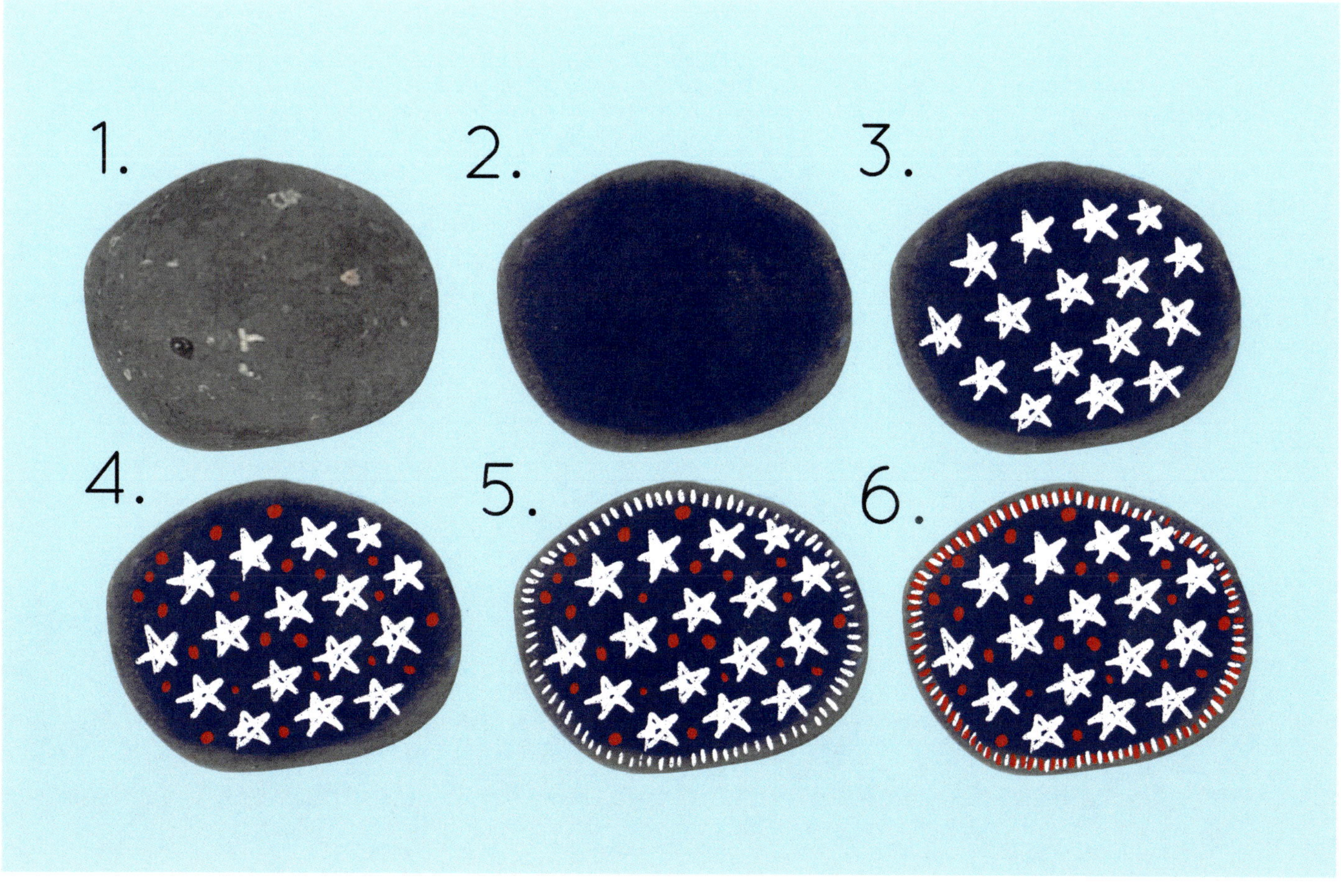

1. 2. 3.

4. 5. 6.

Hearts

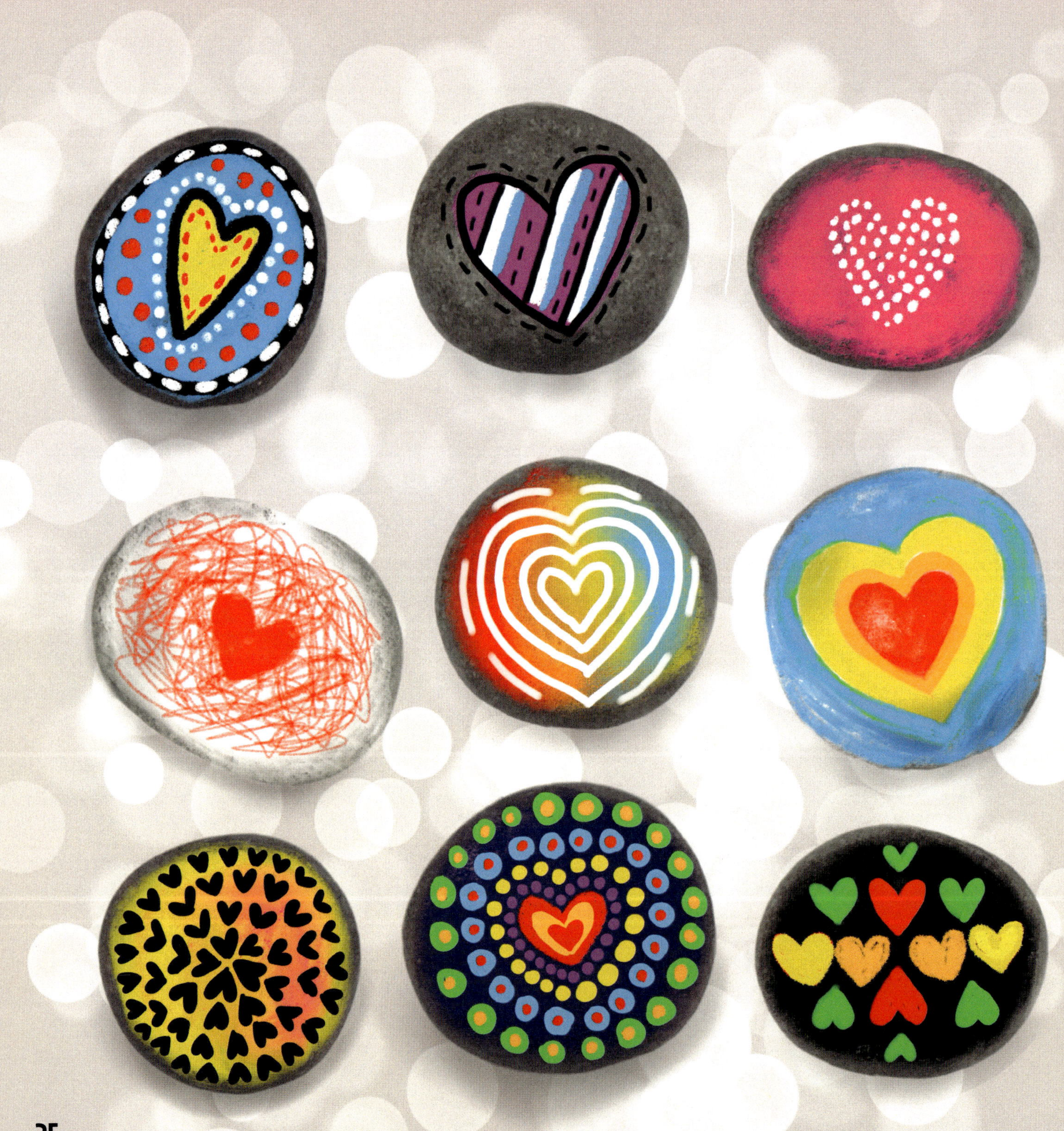

YOU WILL NEED:

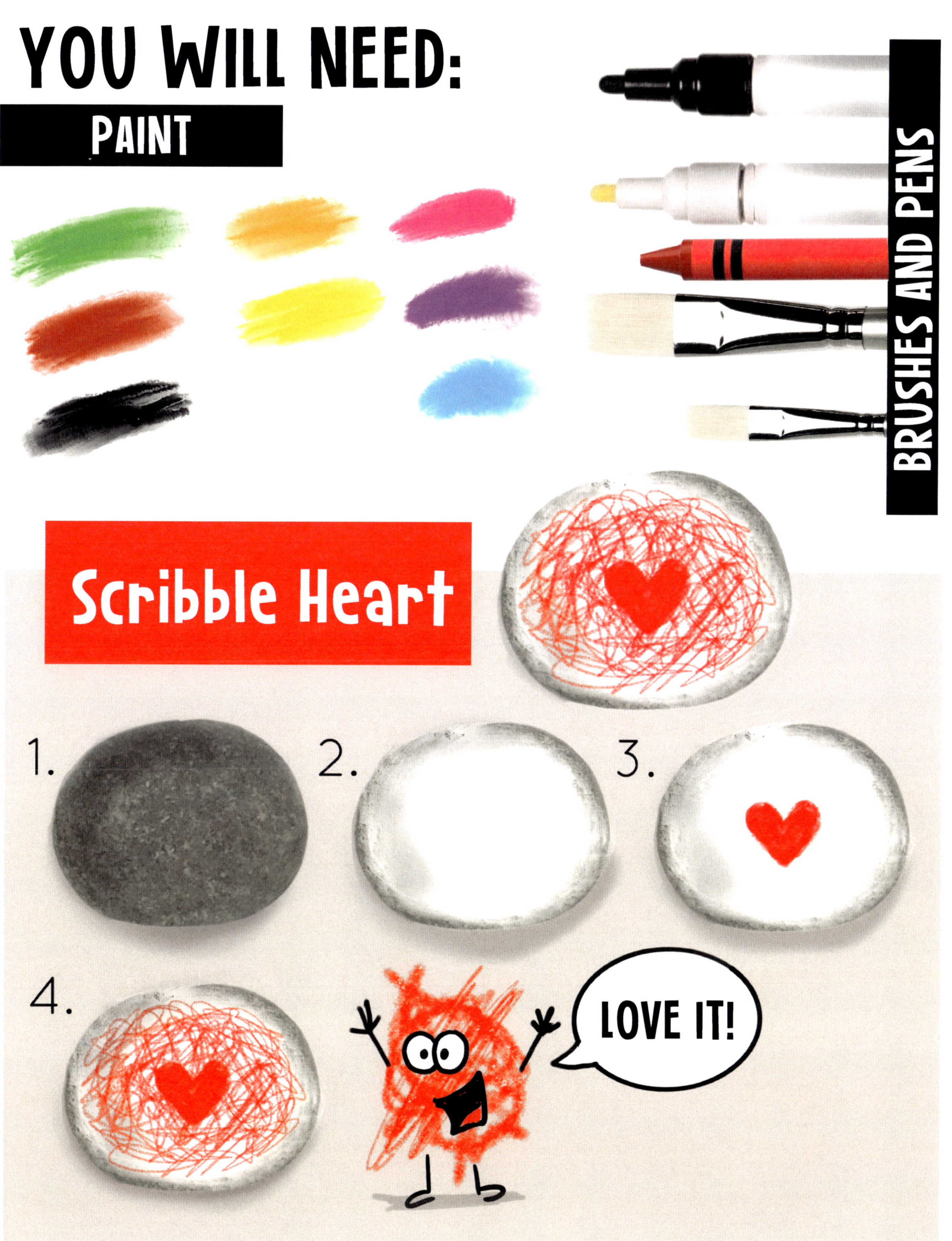

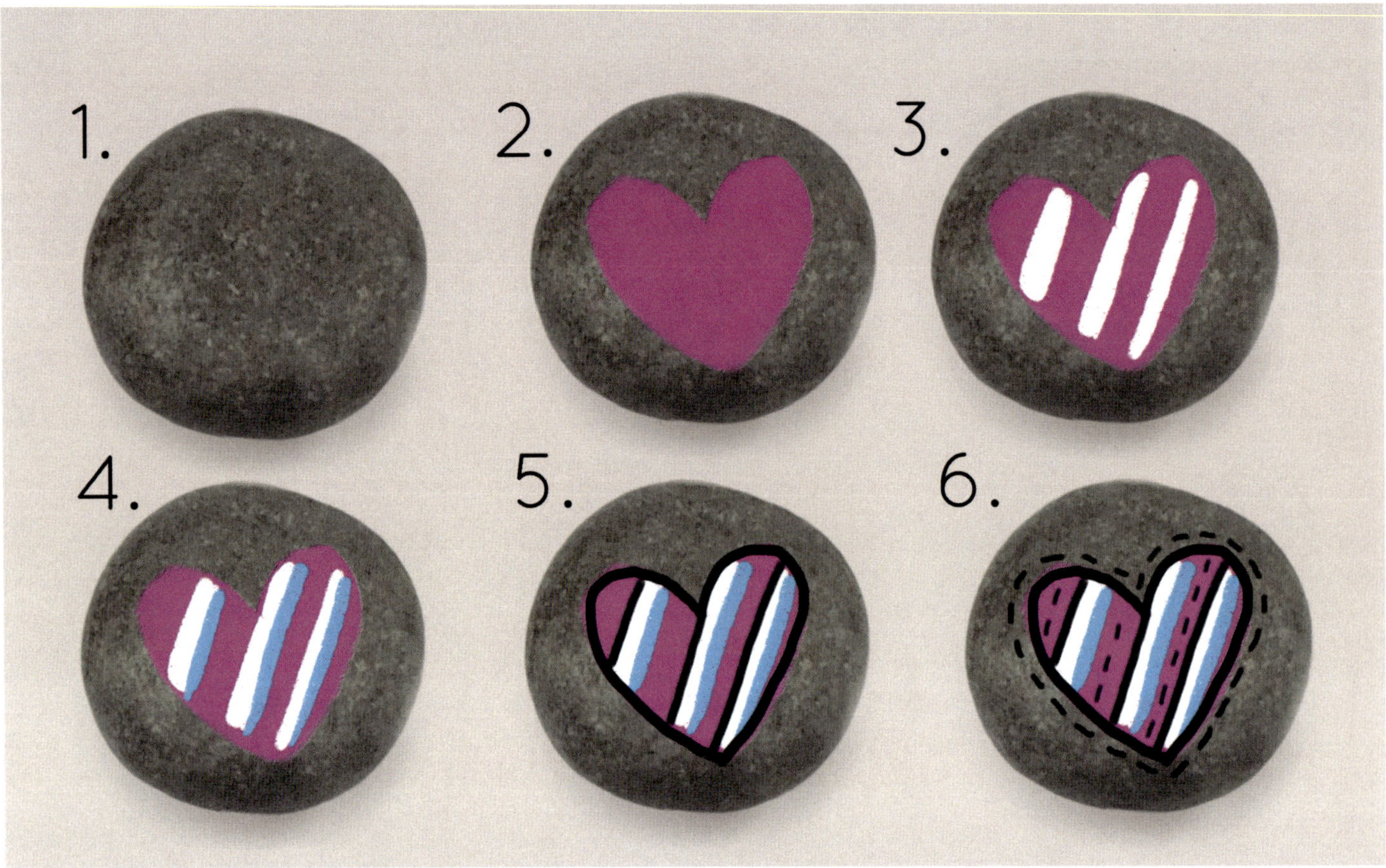

1.

2.

3.

4.

5.

6.

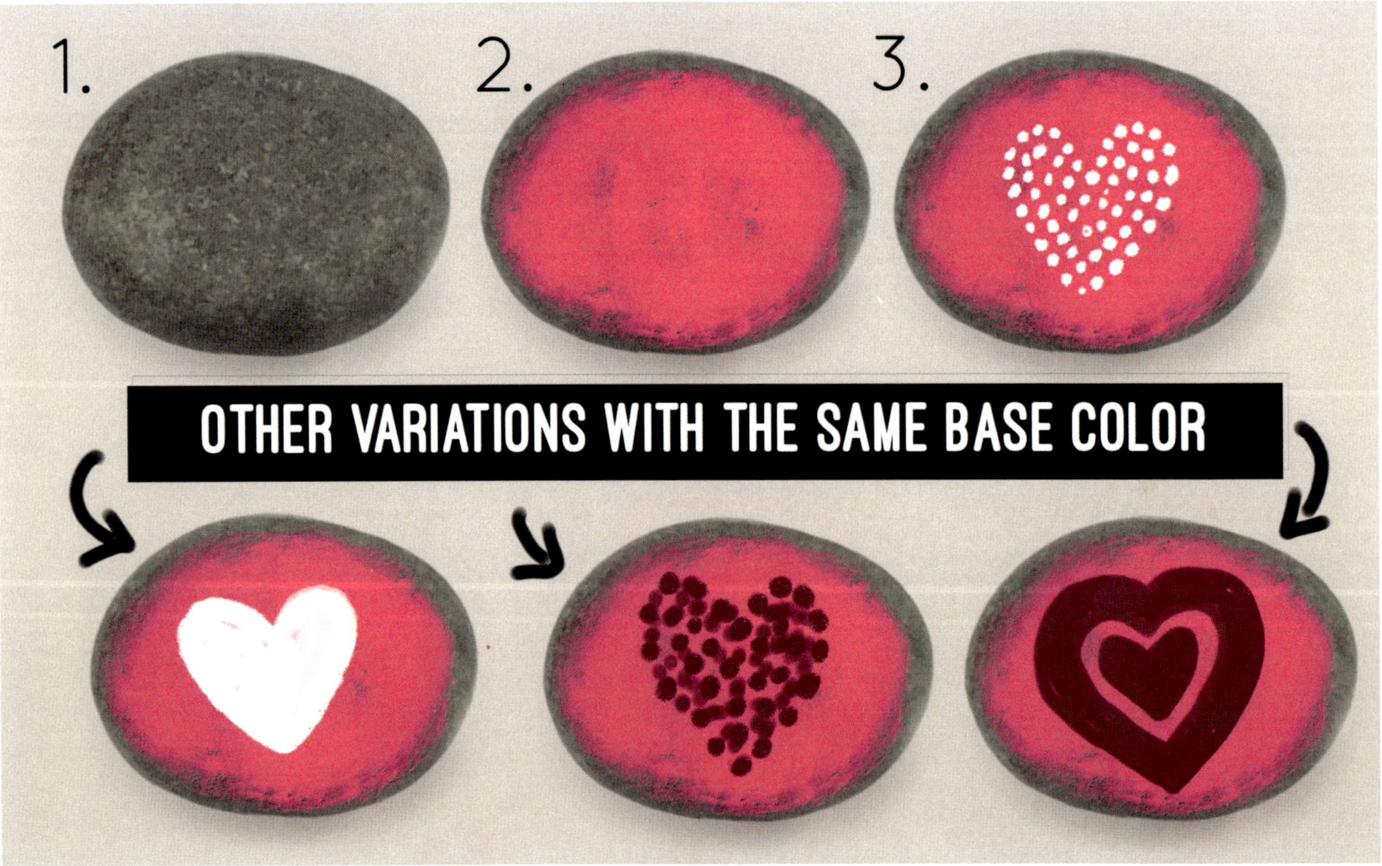

1.

2.

3.

OTHER VARIATIONS WITH THE SAME BASE COLOR

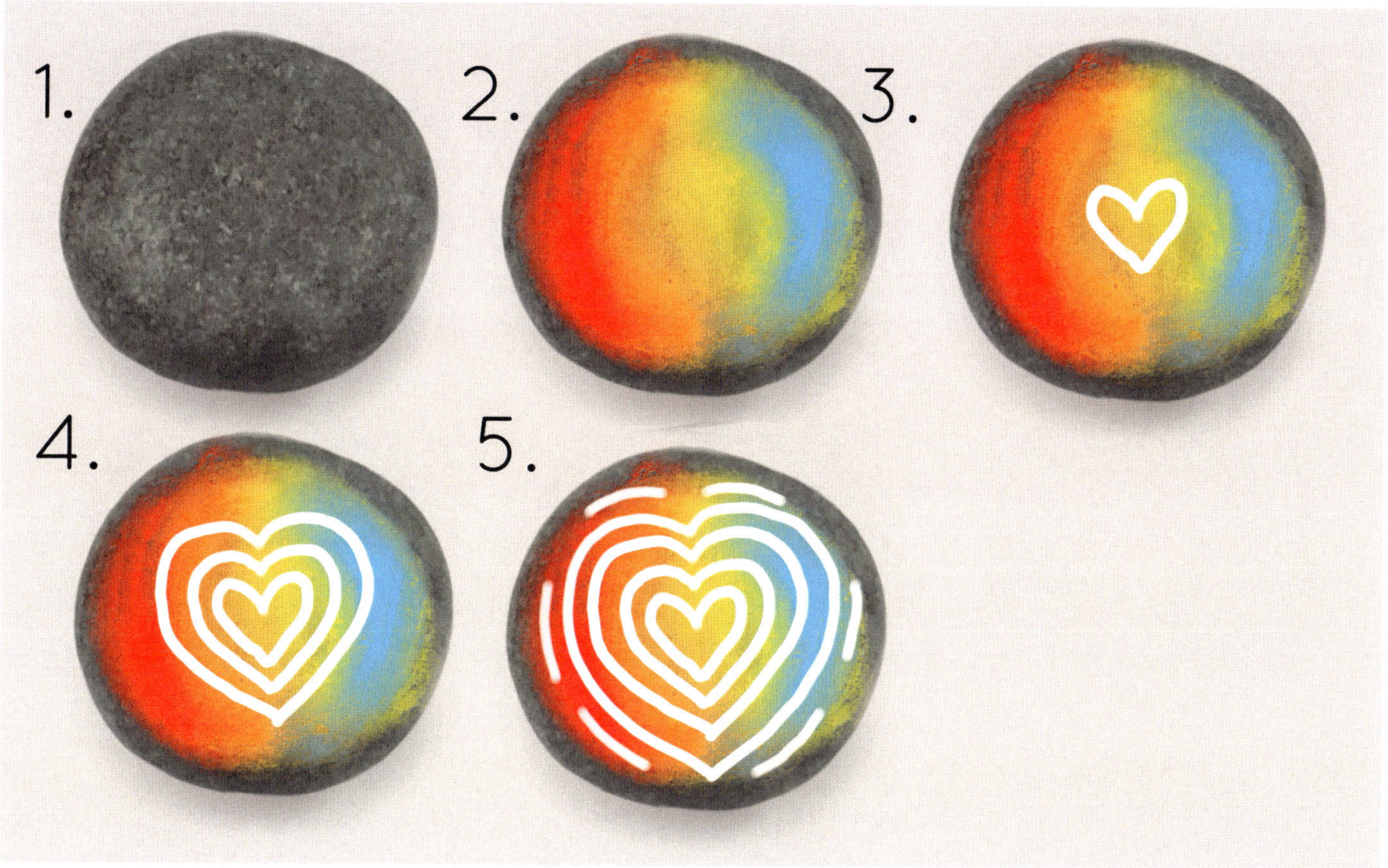

1.

2.

3.

4.

5.

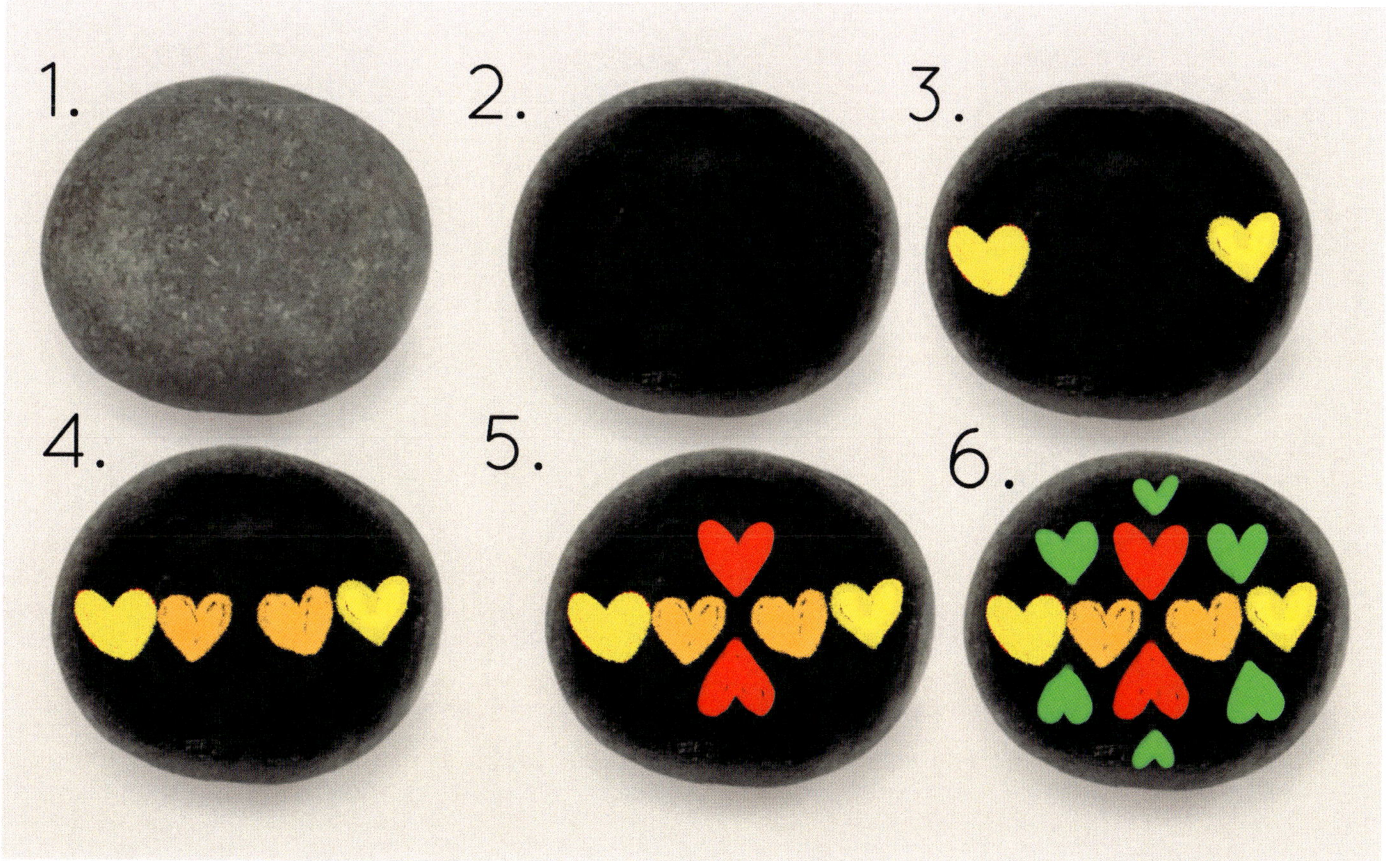

1.

2.

3.

4.

5.

6.

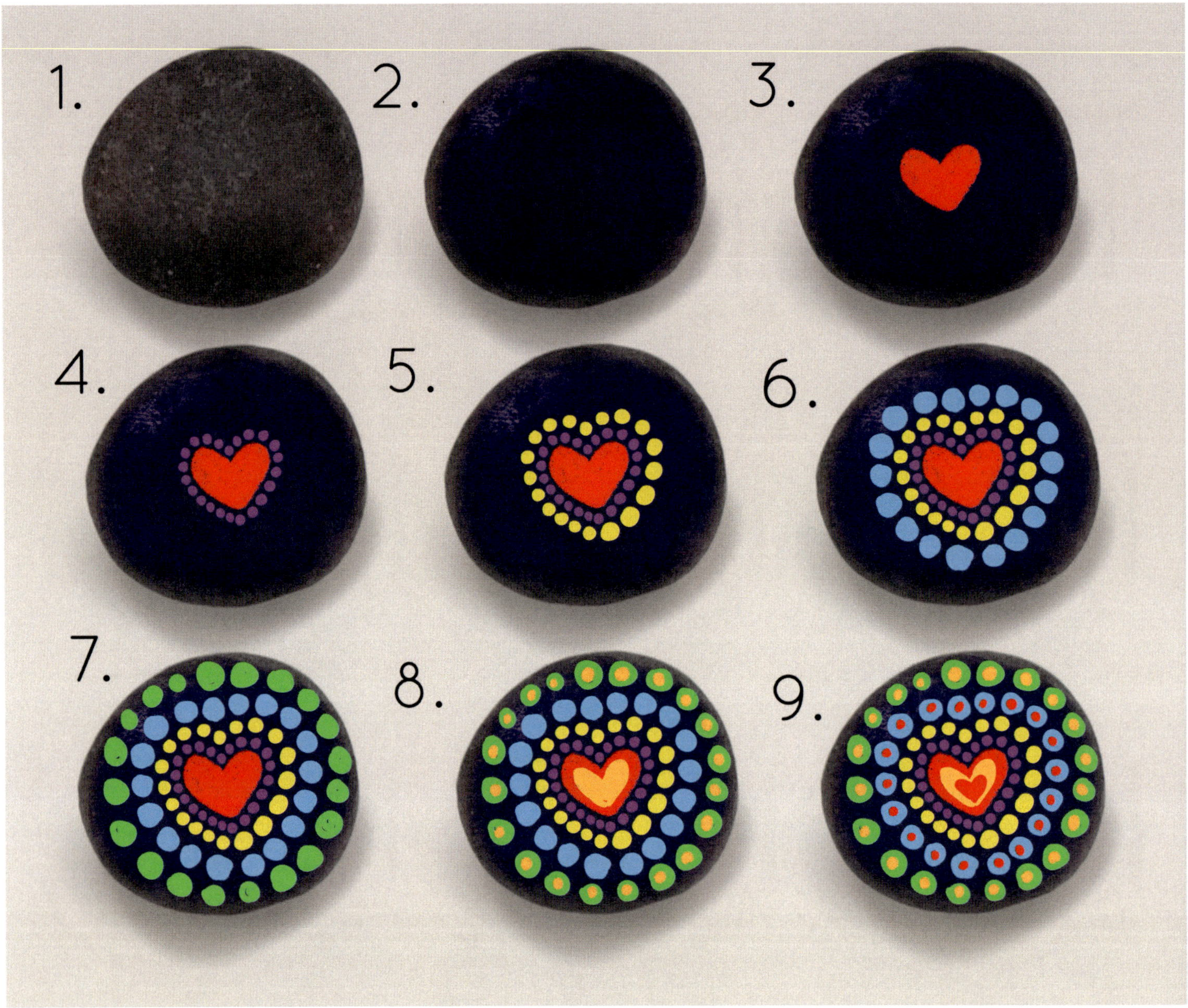

1. 2. 3.

4. 5. 6.

7. 8. 9.

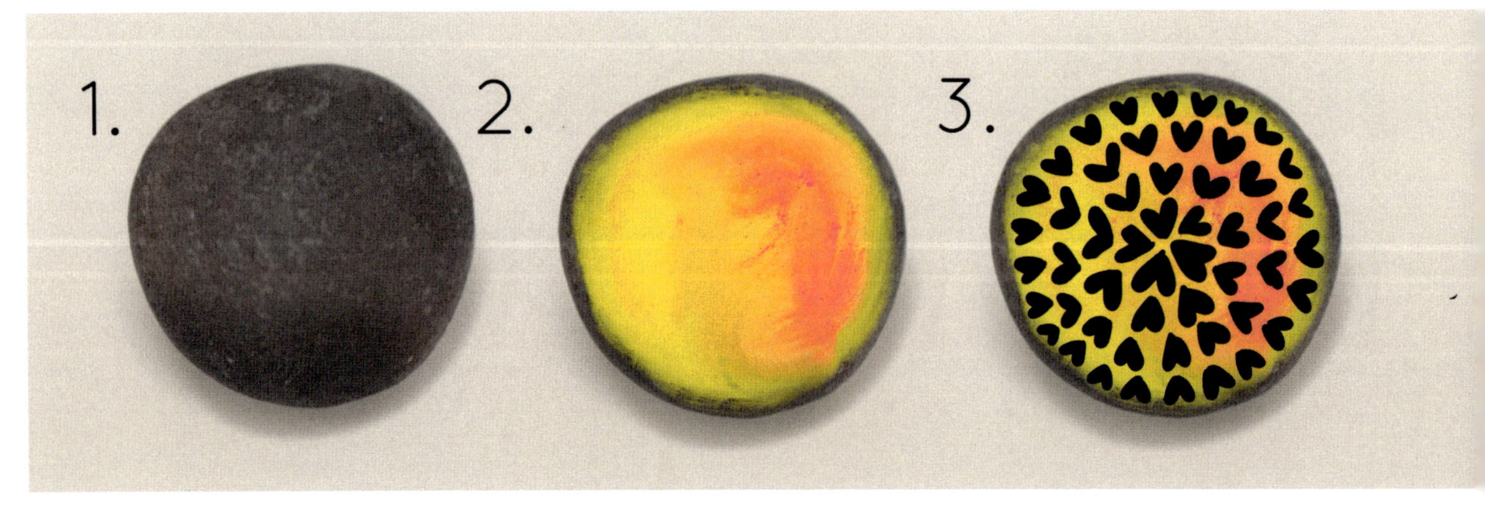

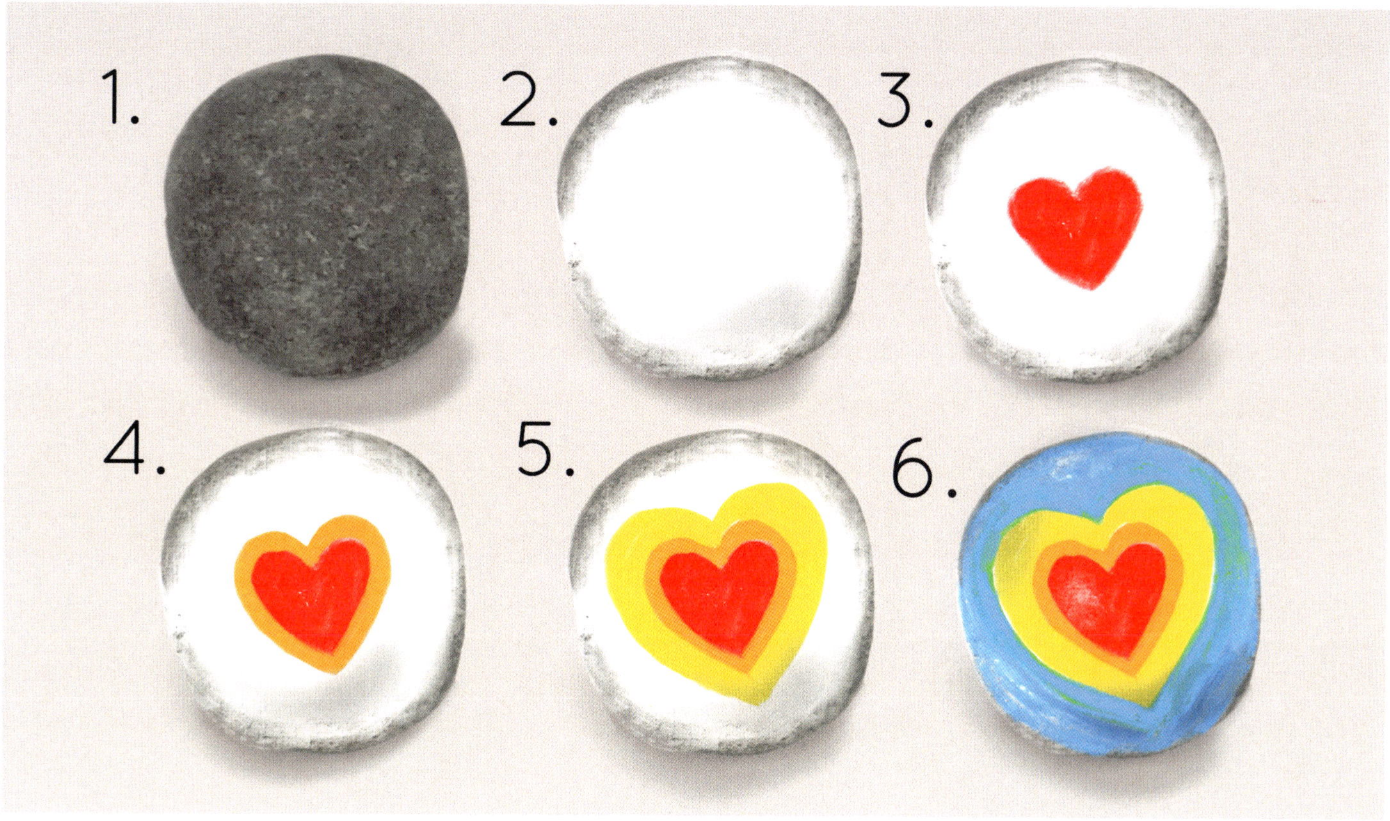

1. 2. 3.

4. 5. 6.

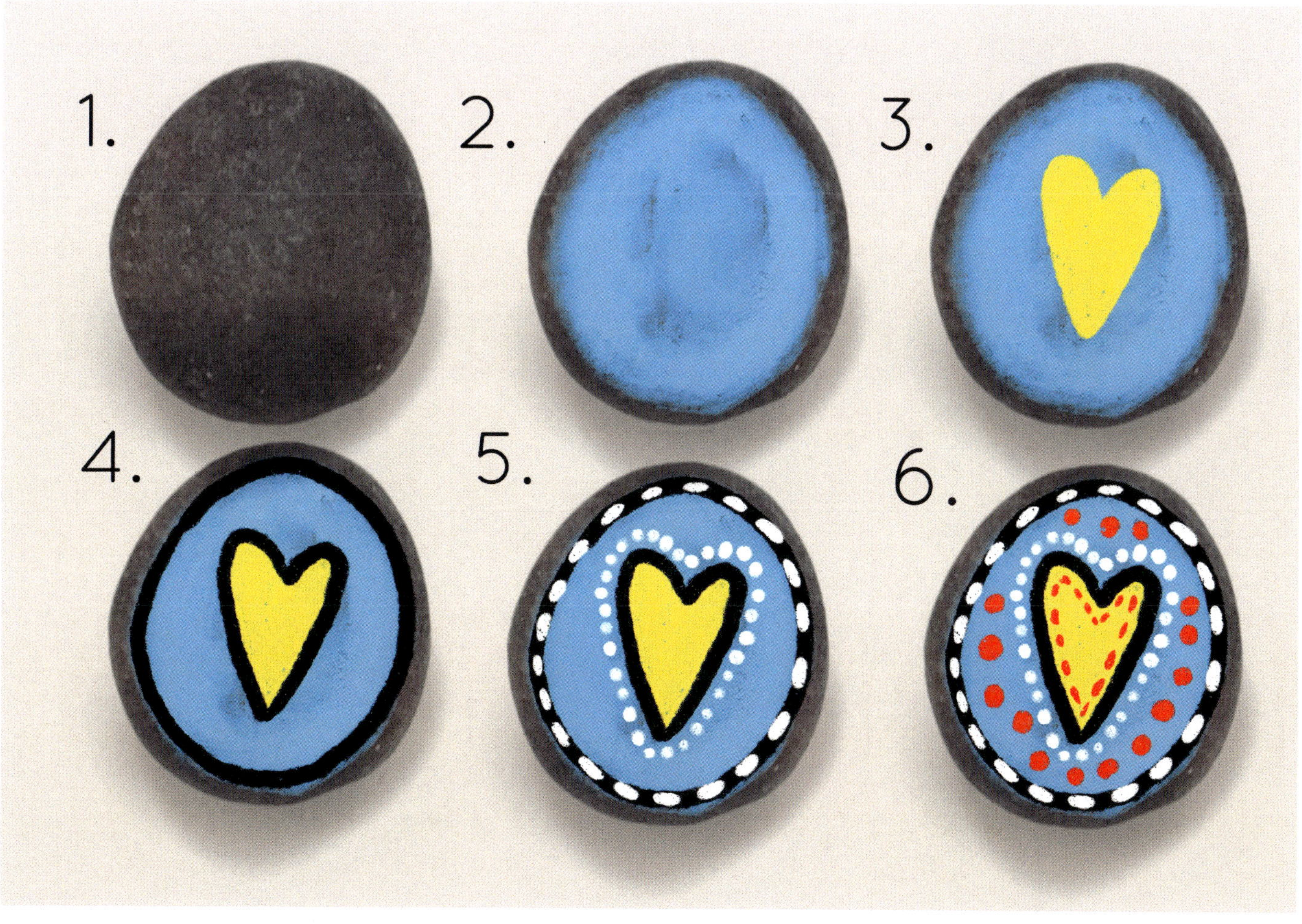

1. 2. 3.

4. 5. 6.

Rainbows and Unicorns

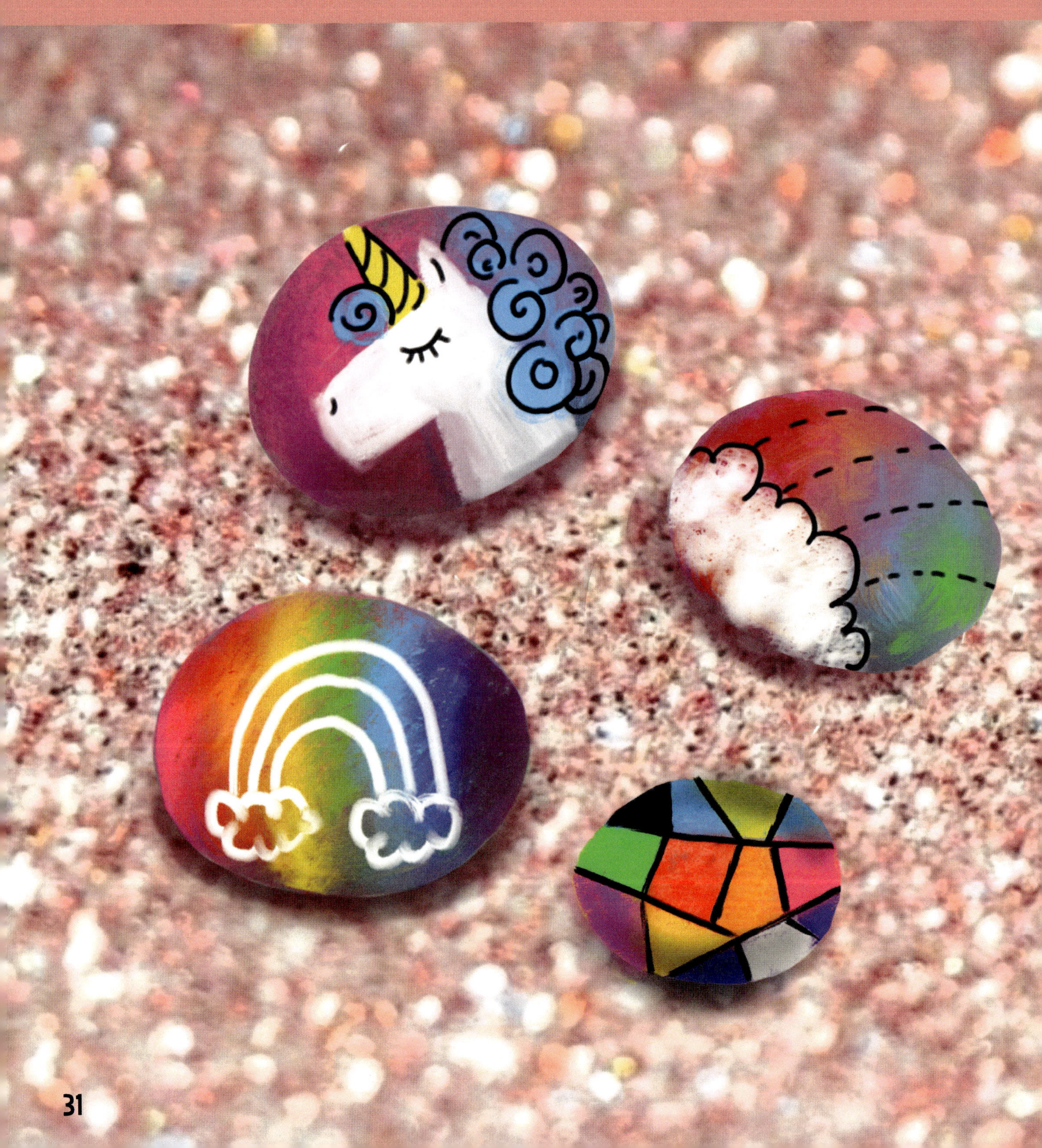

YOU WILL NEED:

PAINT

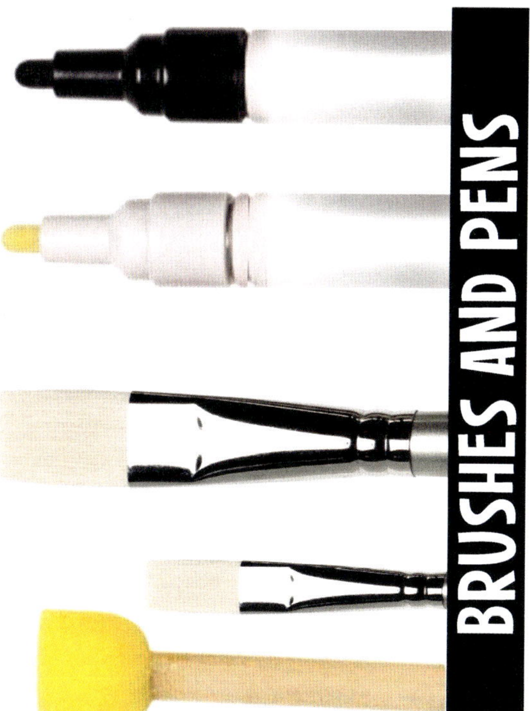

Unicorn

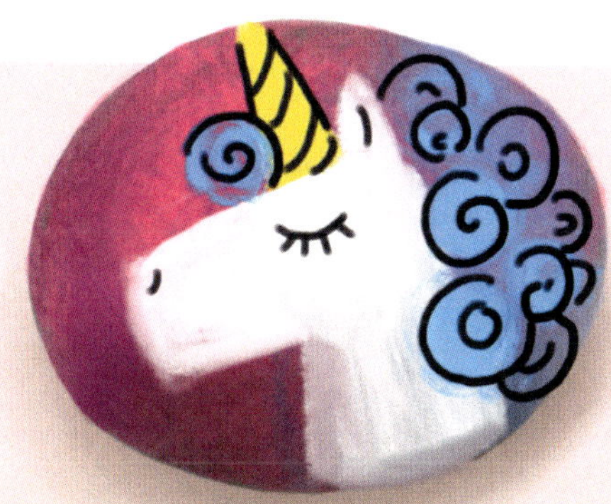

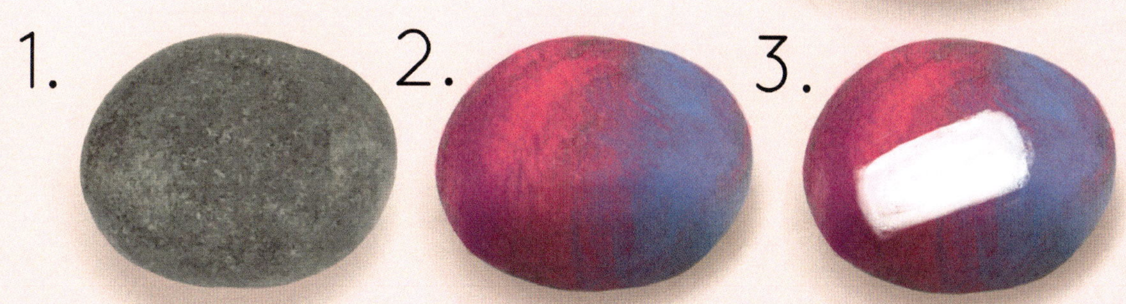

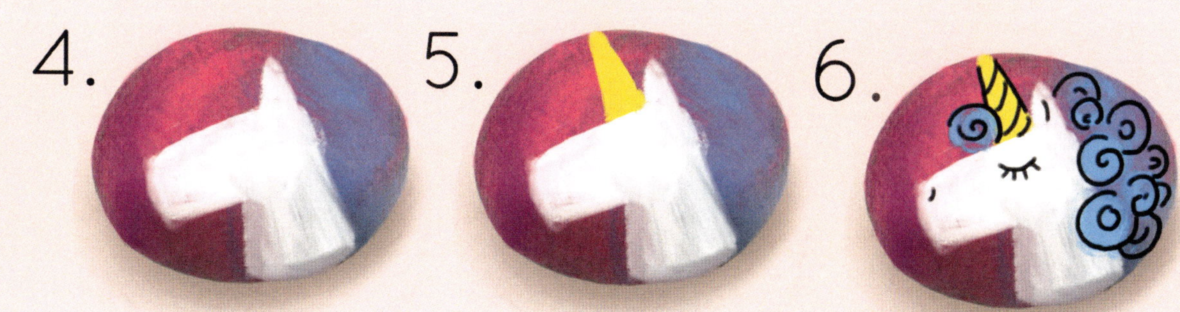

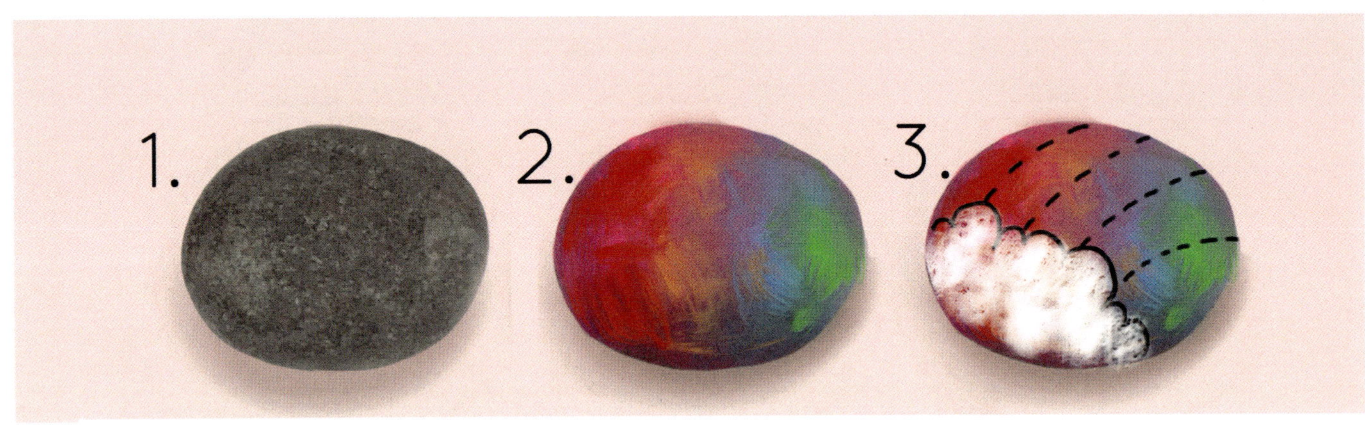

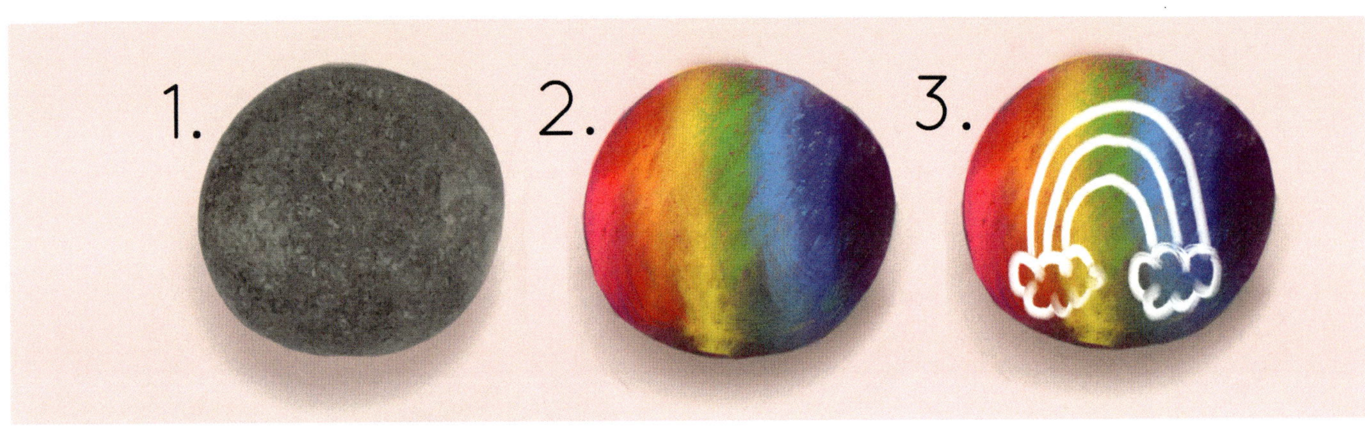

YOU CAN USE A COTTON SWAB TO PAINT DOTS FOR THIS RAINBOW

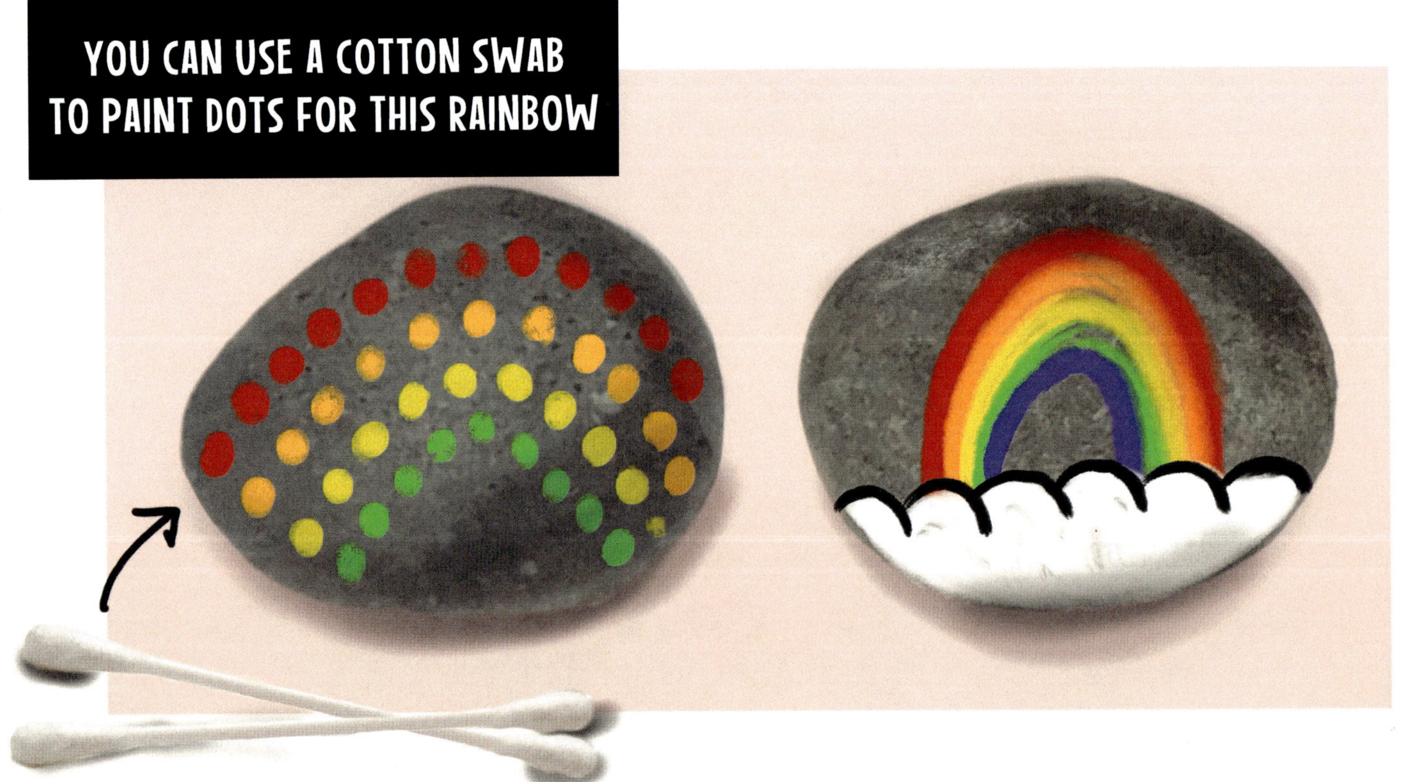

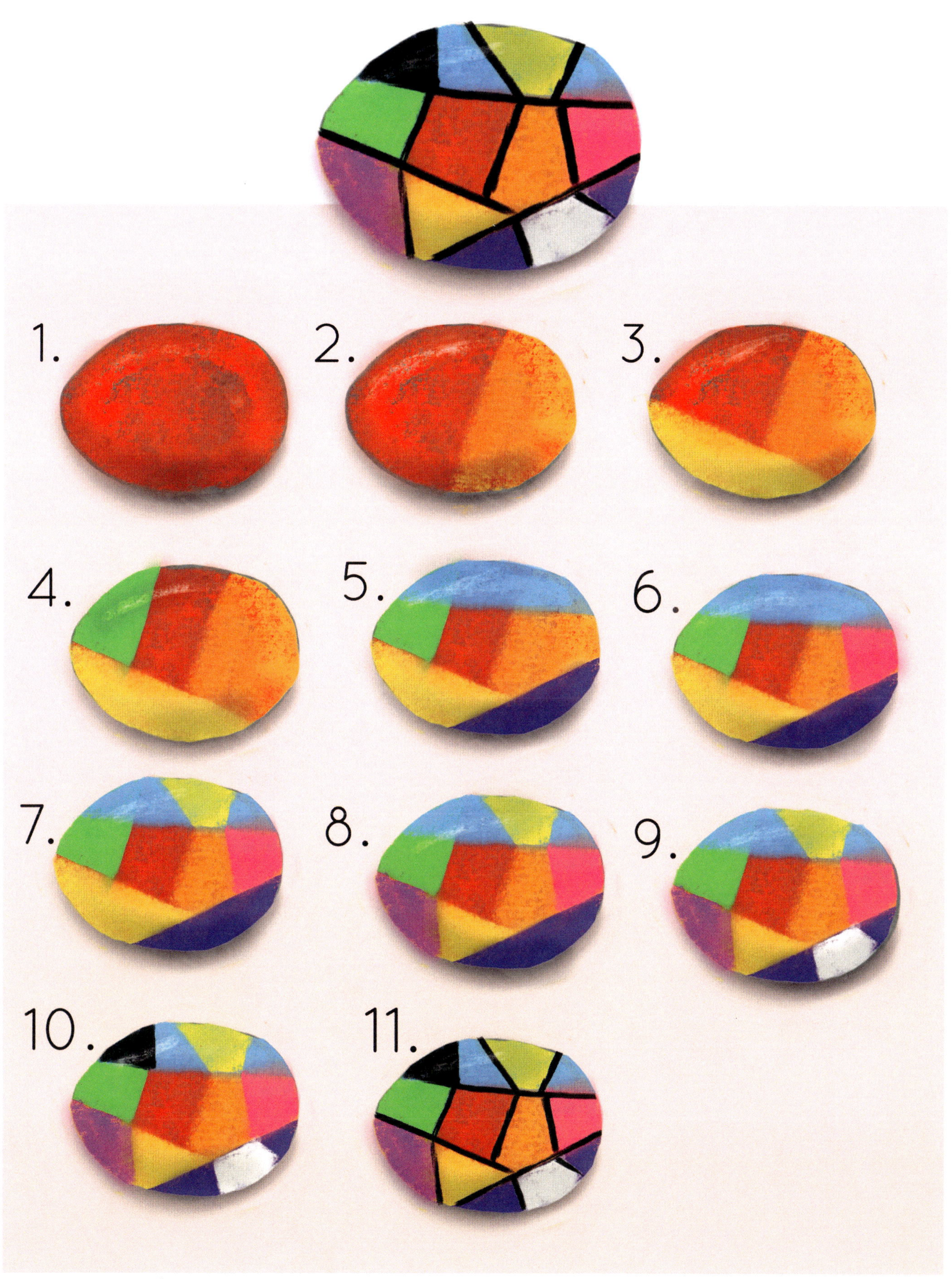
1.
2.
3.
4.
5.
6.
7.
8.
9.
10.
11.

Ocean Stones

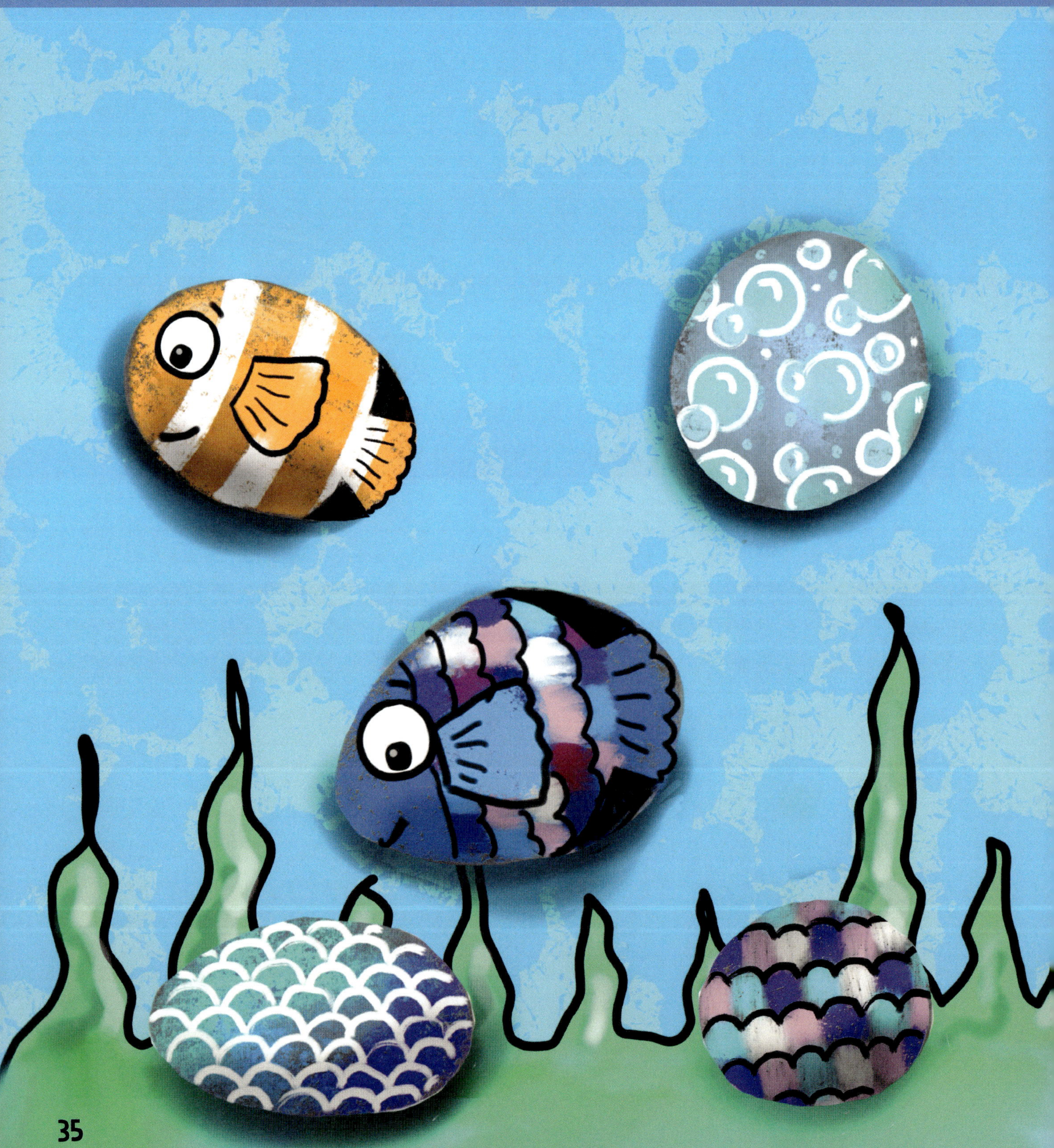

YOU WILL NEED:

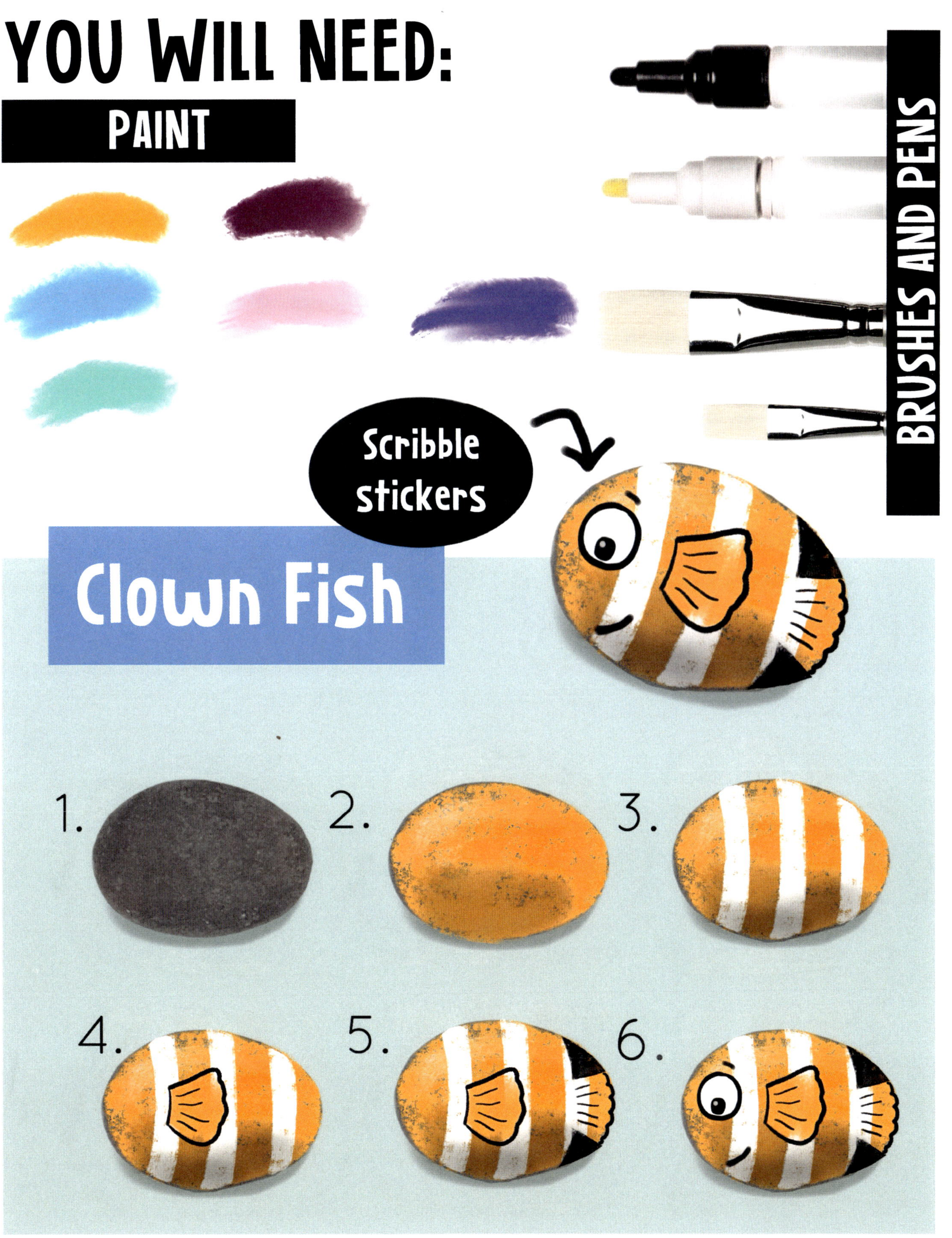

Clown Fish

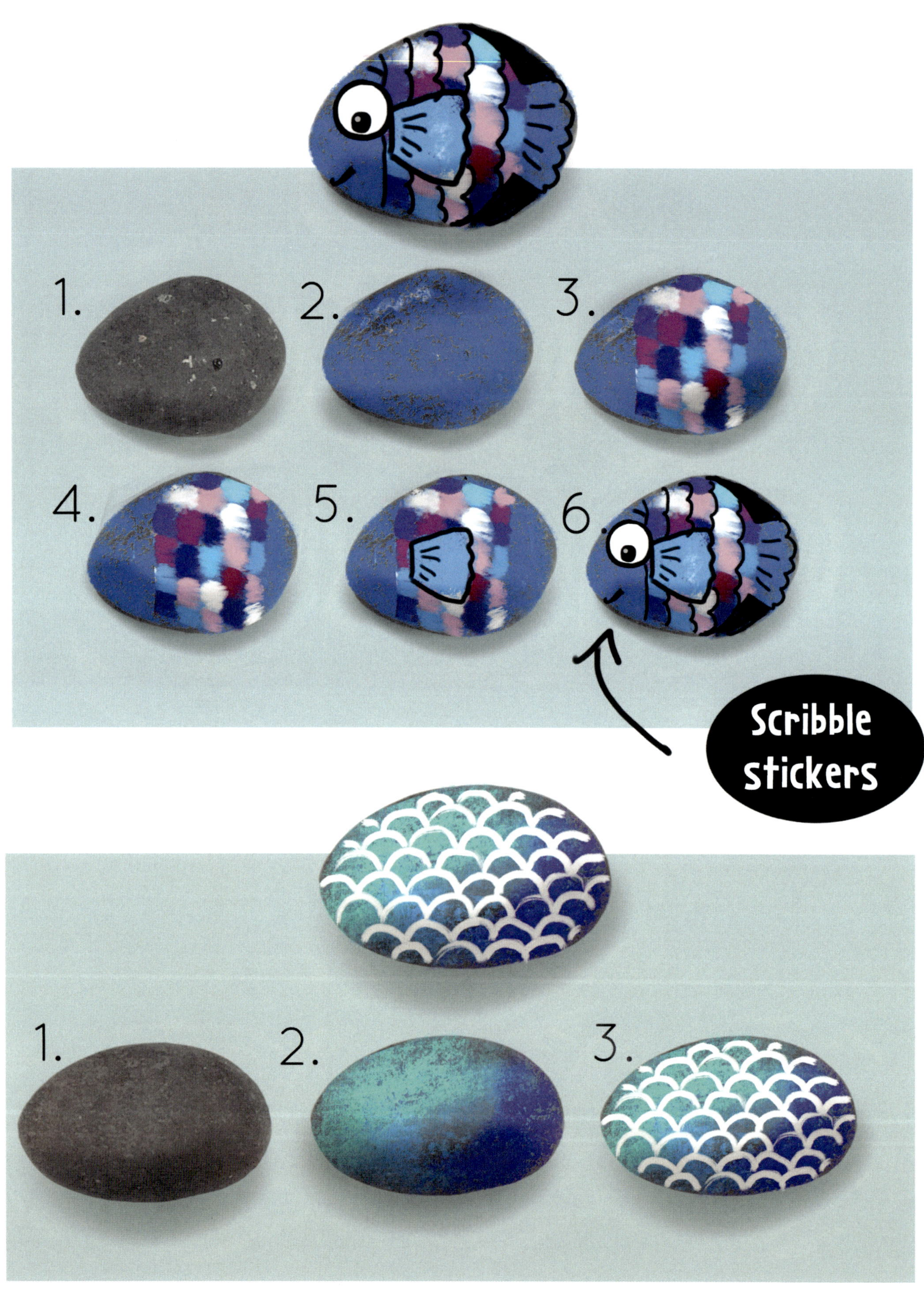
1.
2.
3.
4.
5.
6.
Scribble stickers
1.
2.
3.

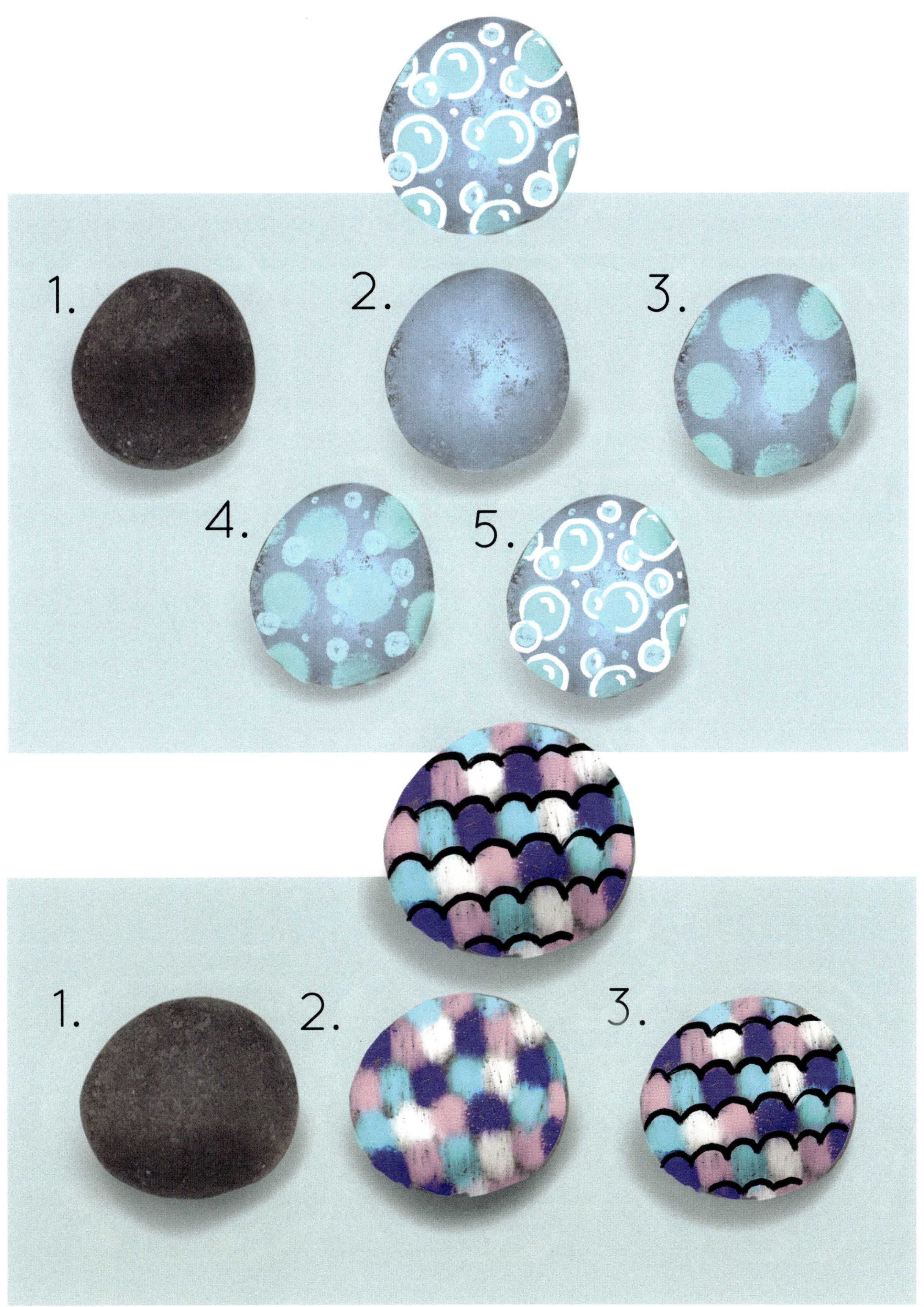
1.
2.
3.
4.
5.
1.
2.
3.

Desert Stones

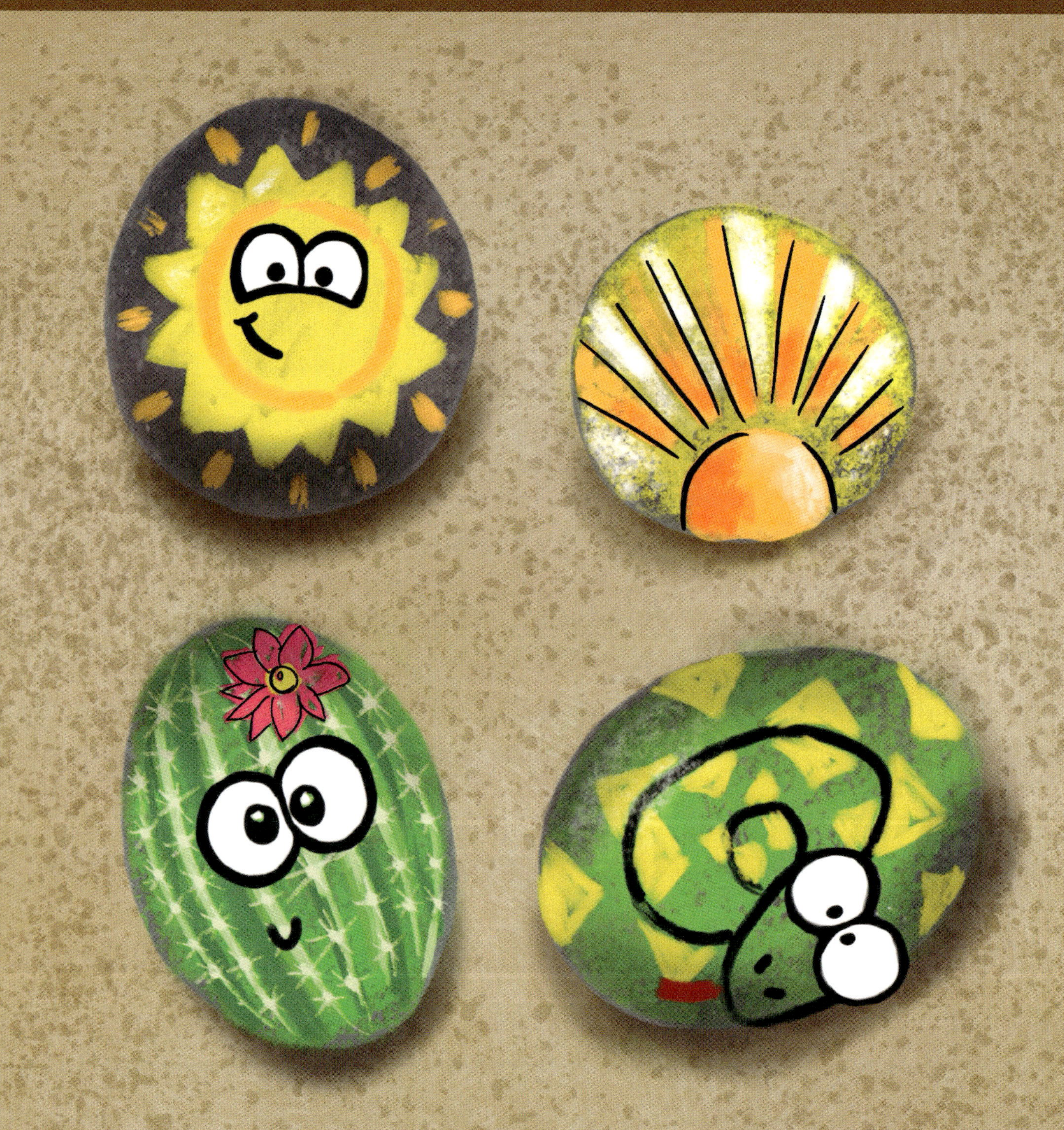

YOU WILL NEED:

PAINT

BRUSHES AND PENS

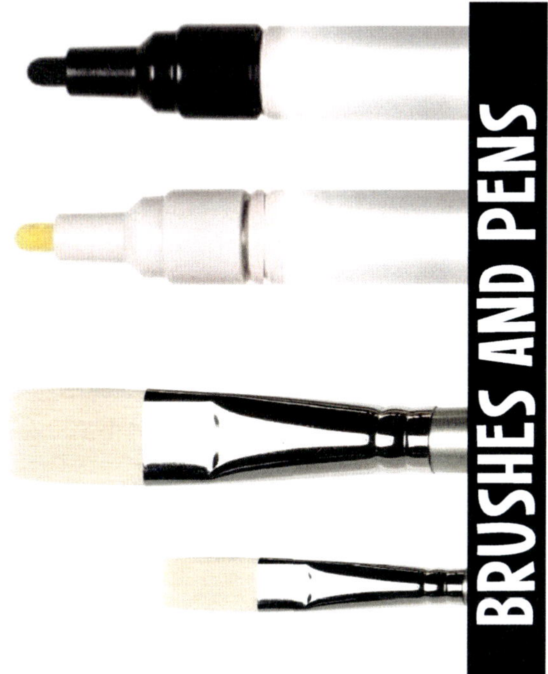

Snake

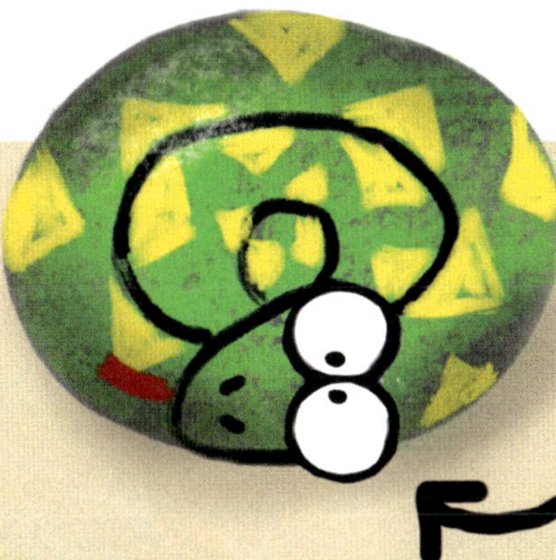

Scribble stickers

1. 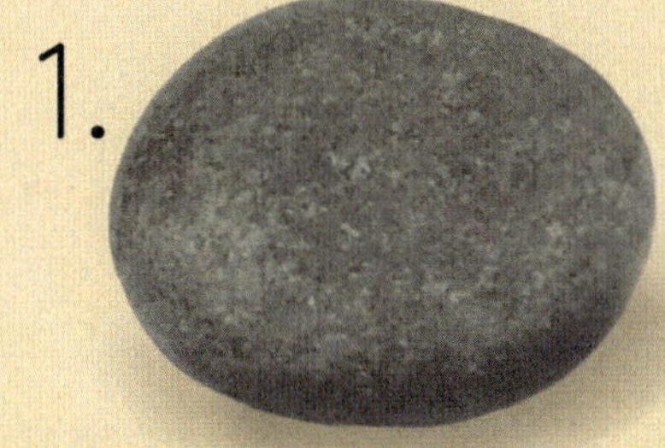

2. 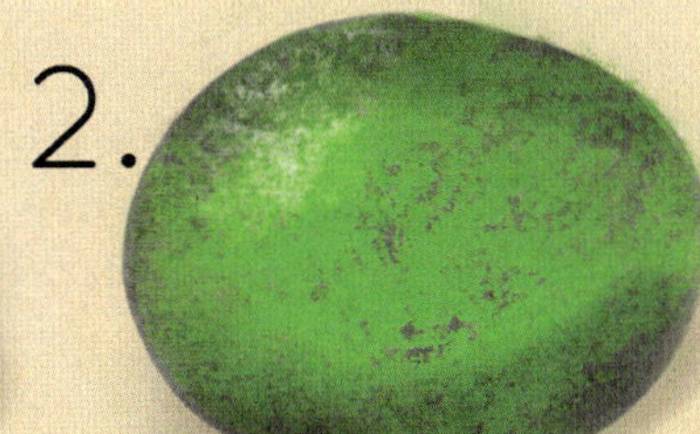

3. 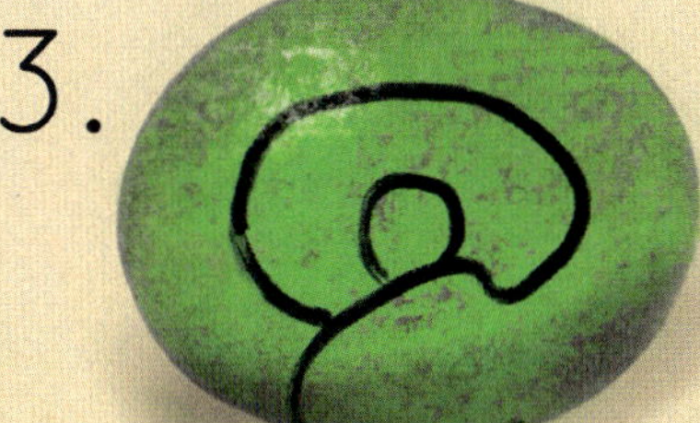

4. 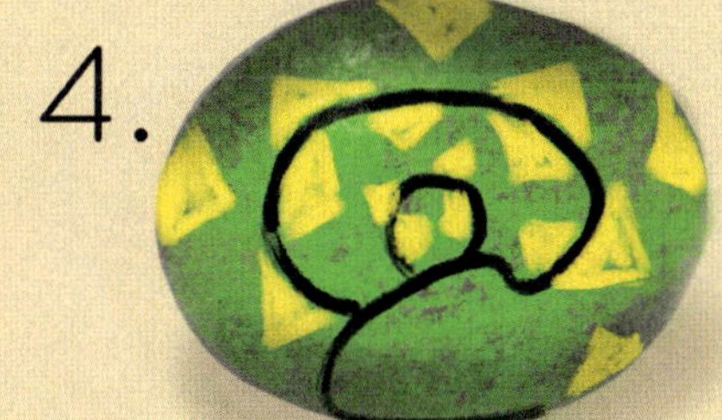

5. 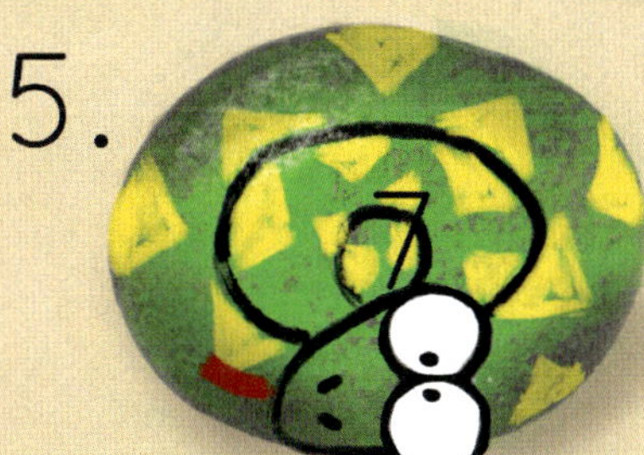

Sunrise

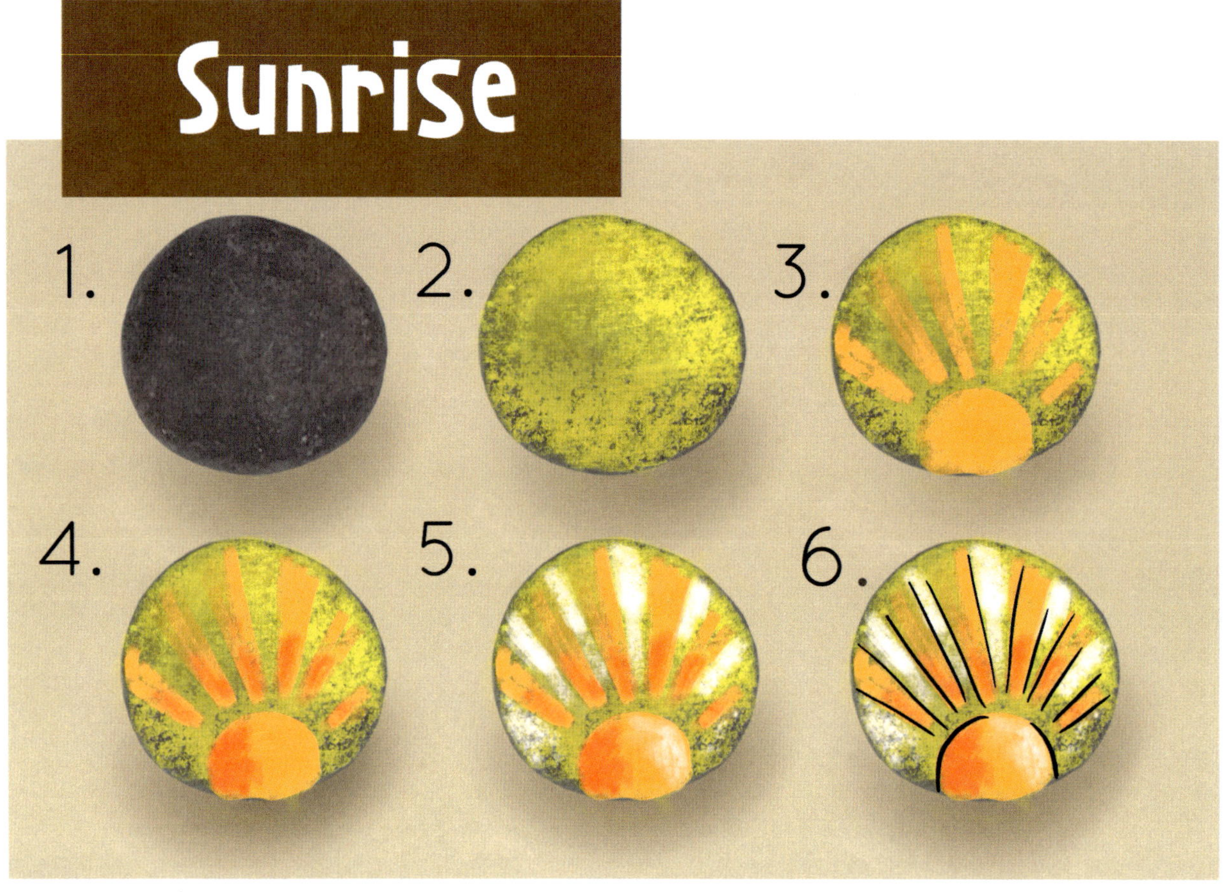

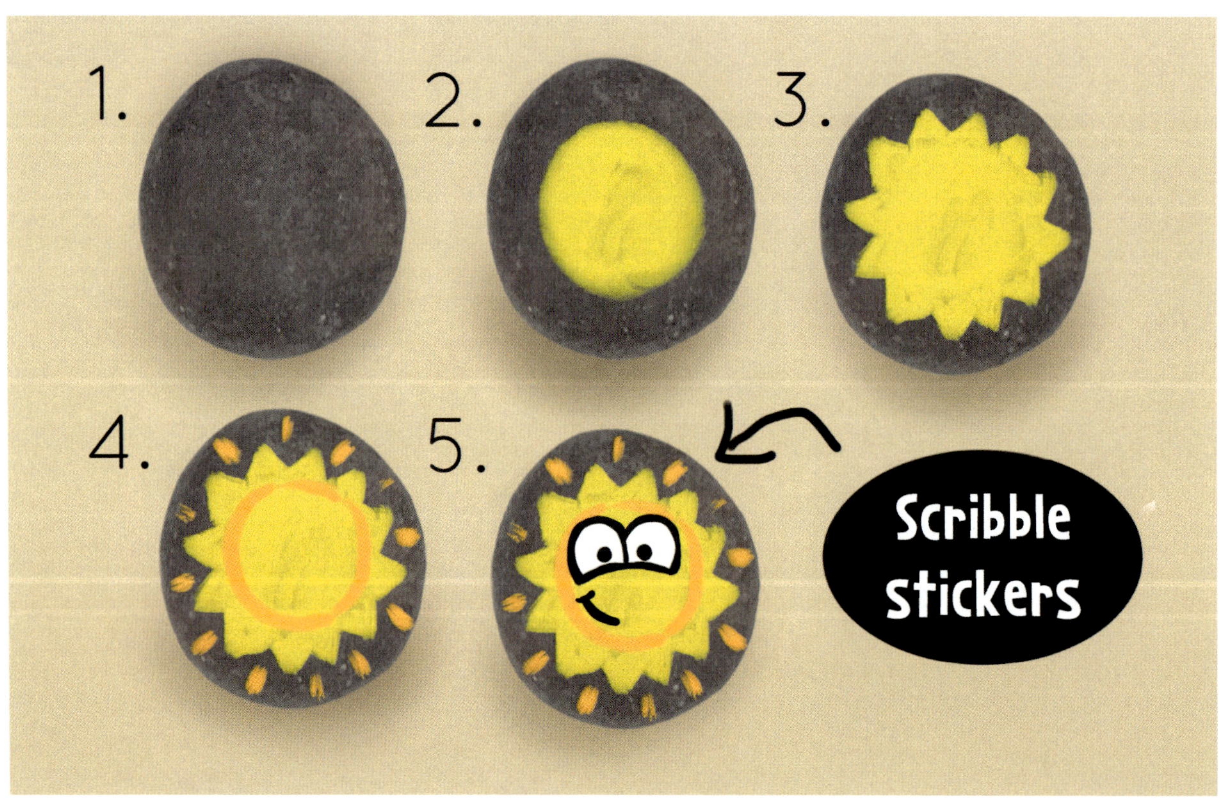

Cactus

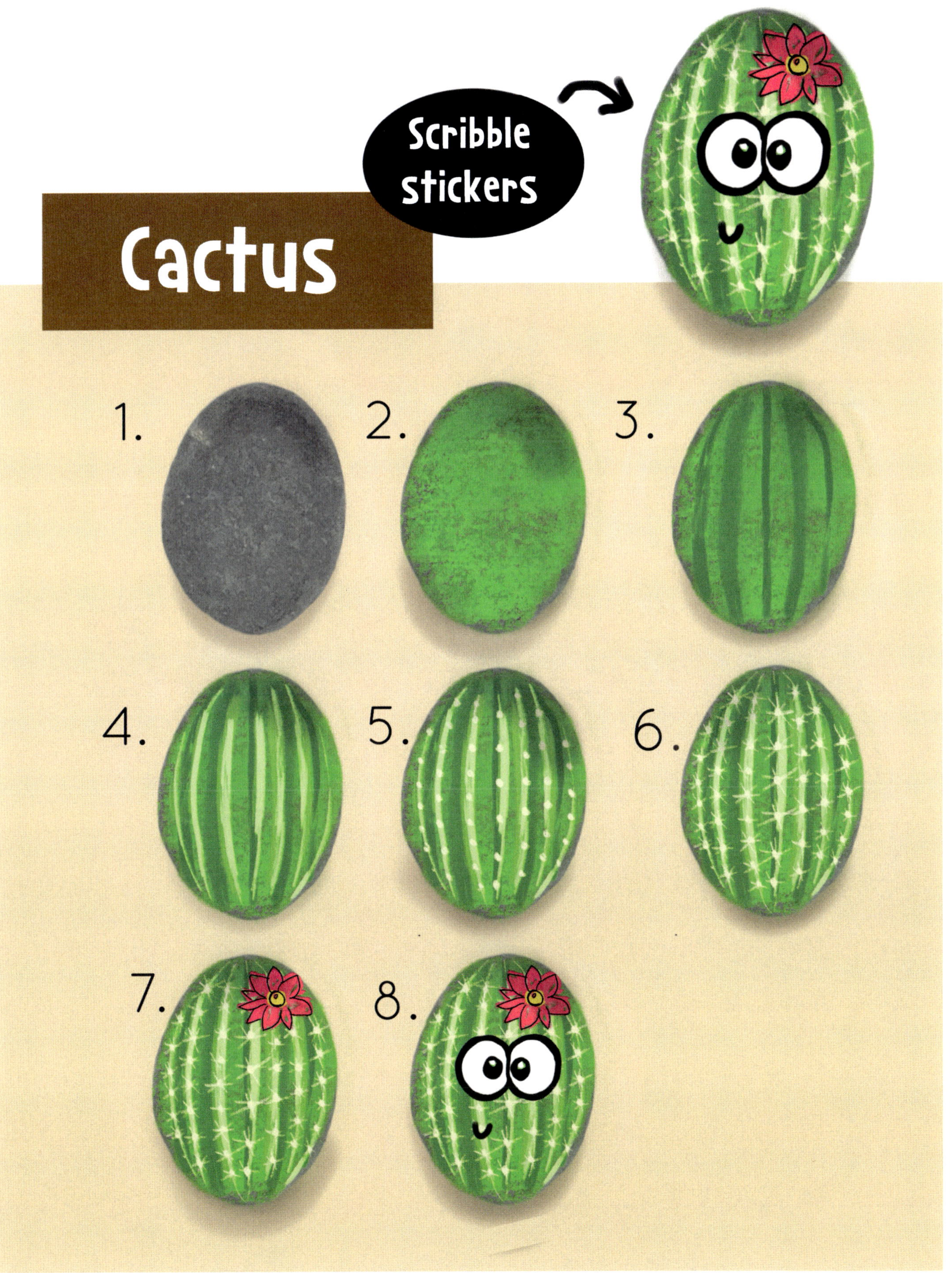

Chilly Stones

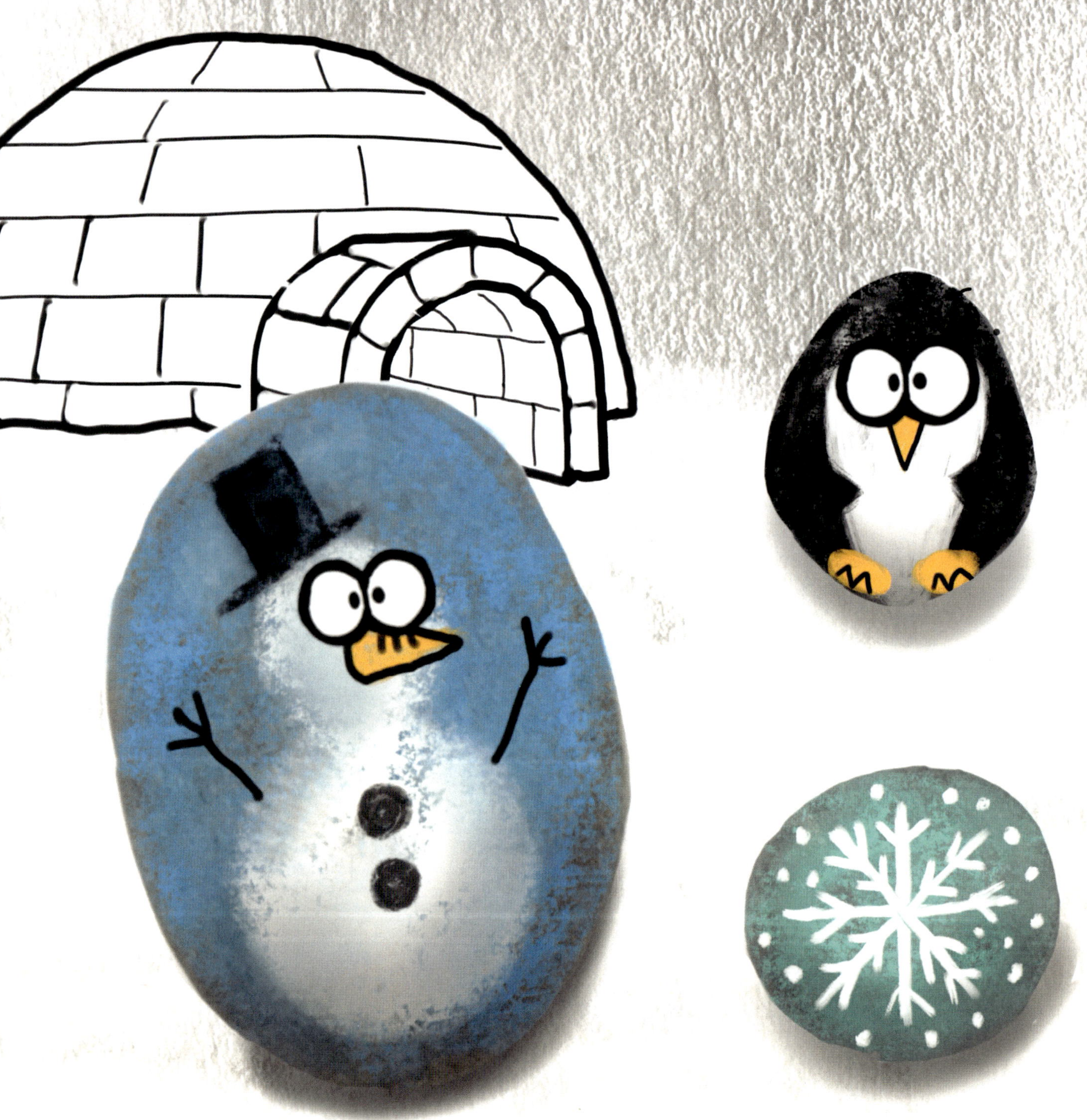

YOU WILL NEED:

PAINT

BRUSHES AND PENS

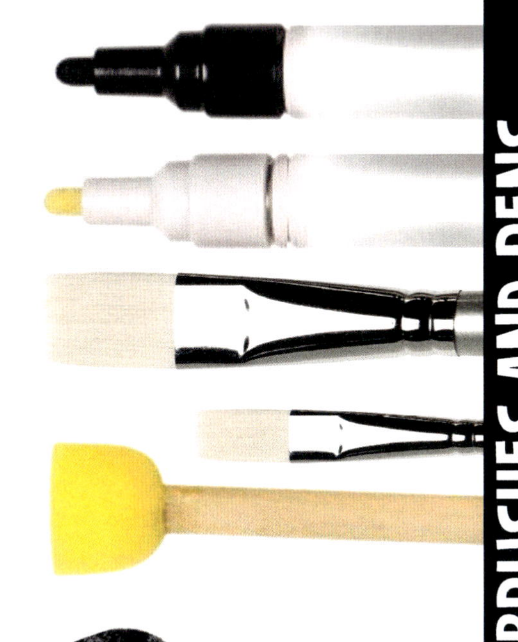

Penguin

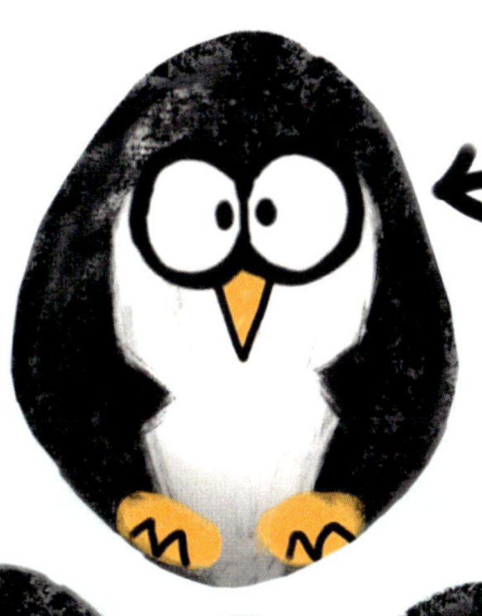

Scribble stickers

1.

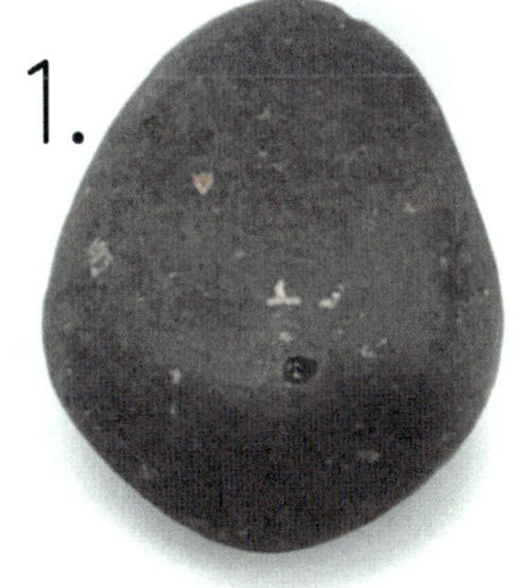

2.

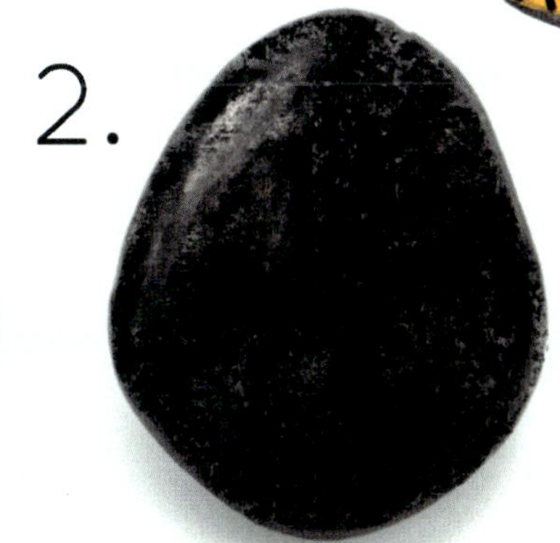

3.

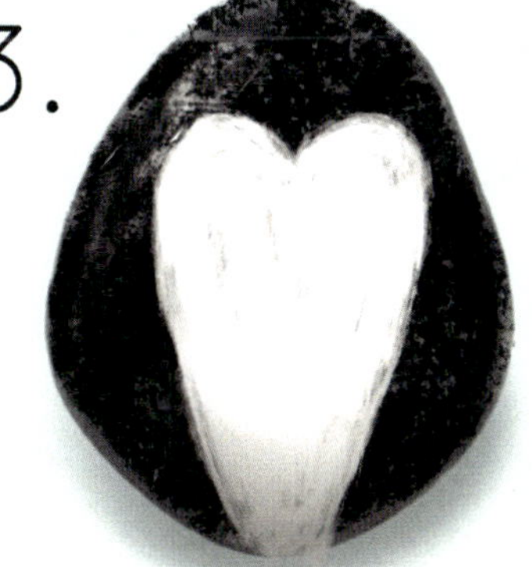

4.

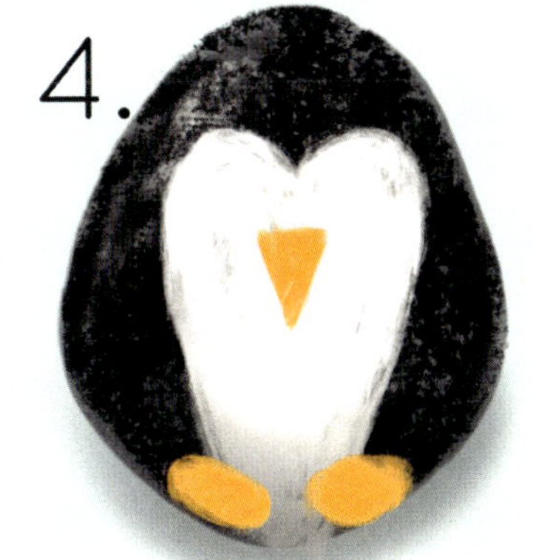

5.

6.

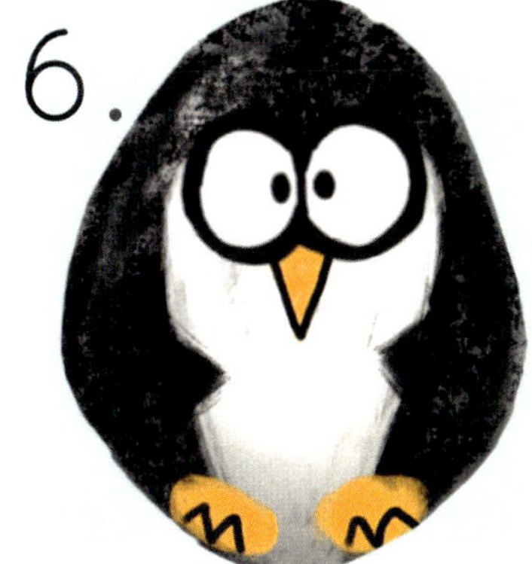

Snowflake

1.

2.

3.

4.

5.

OTHER VARIATIONS

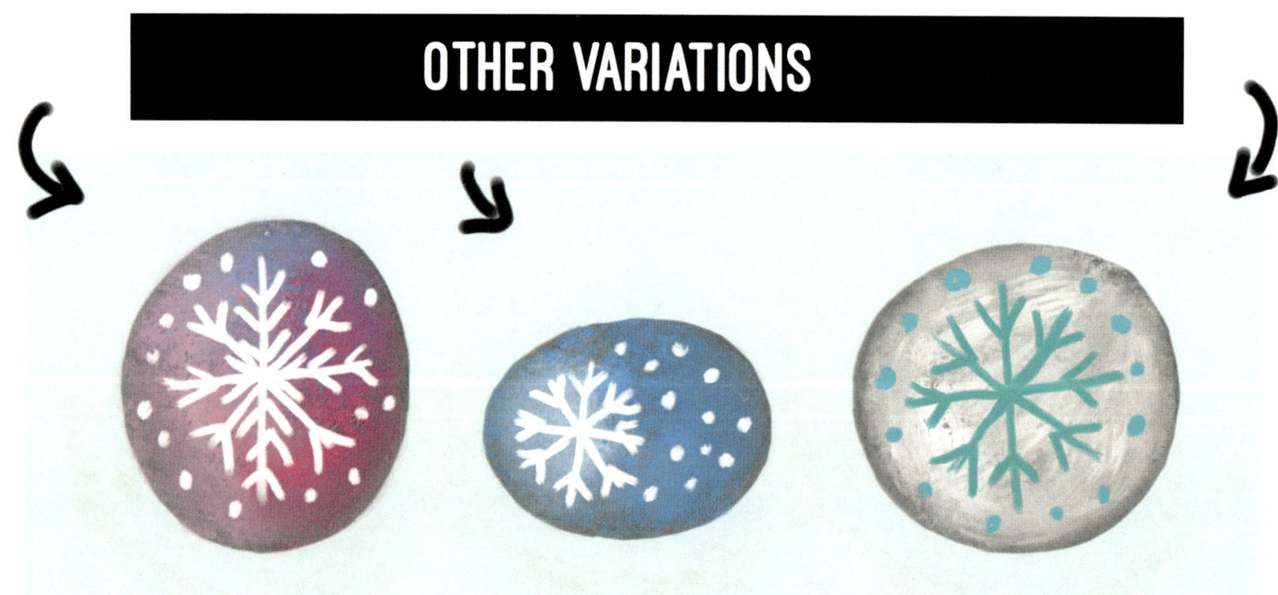

Snowman

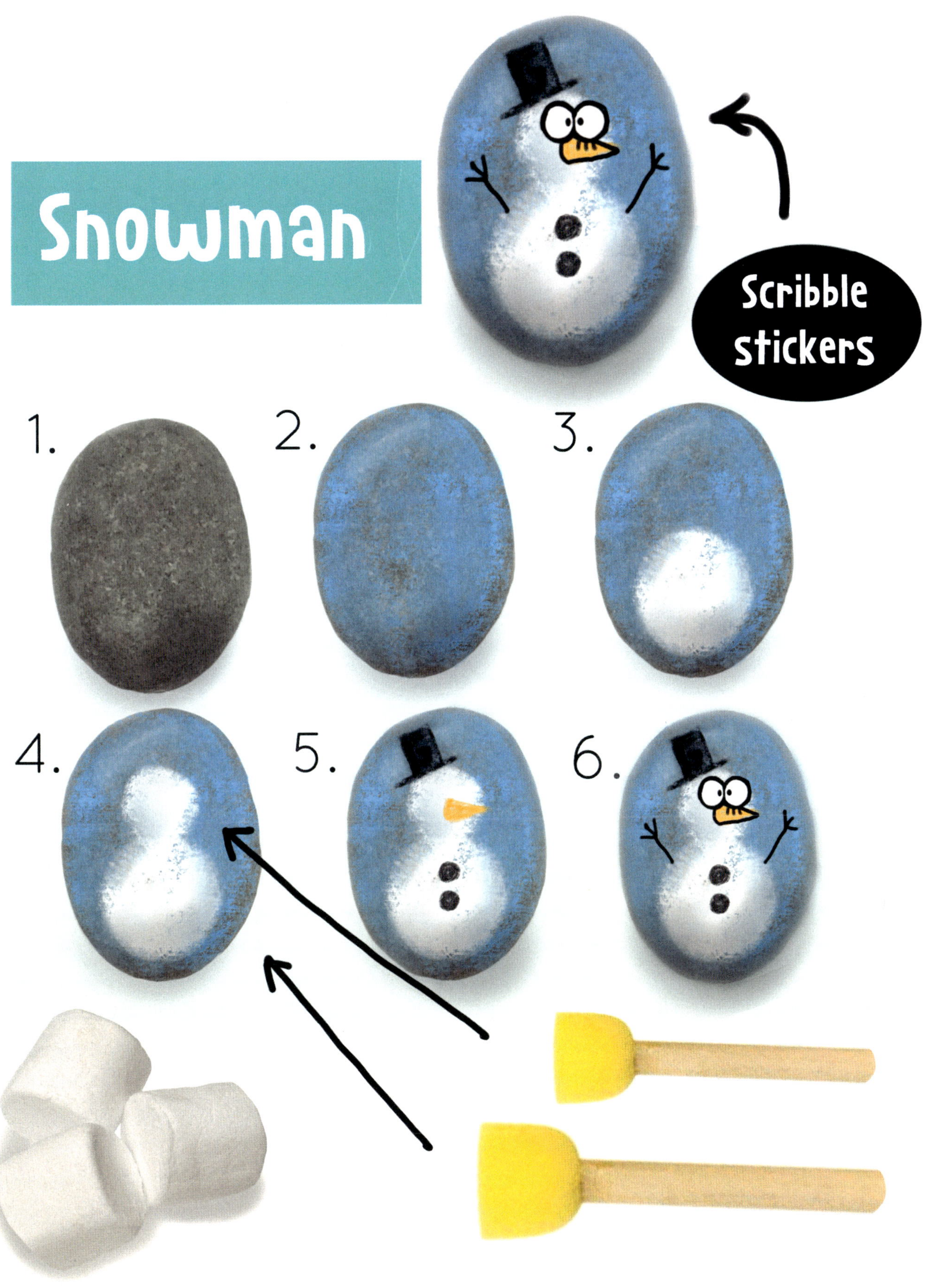

Flowers and leaves

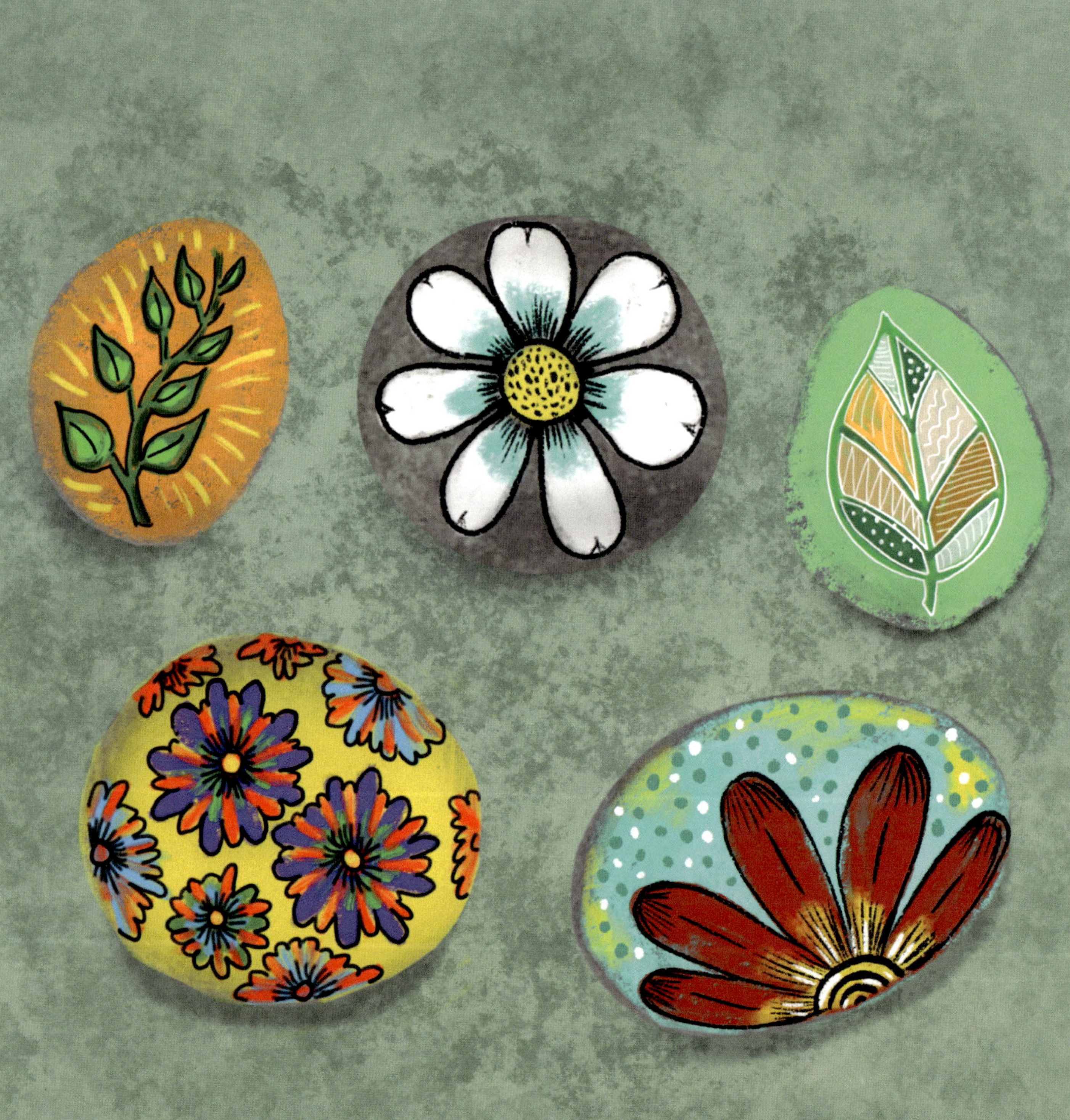

YOU WILL NEED:

PAINT

BRUSHES AND PENS

Daisy

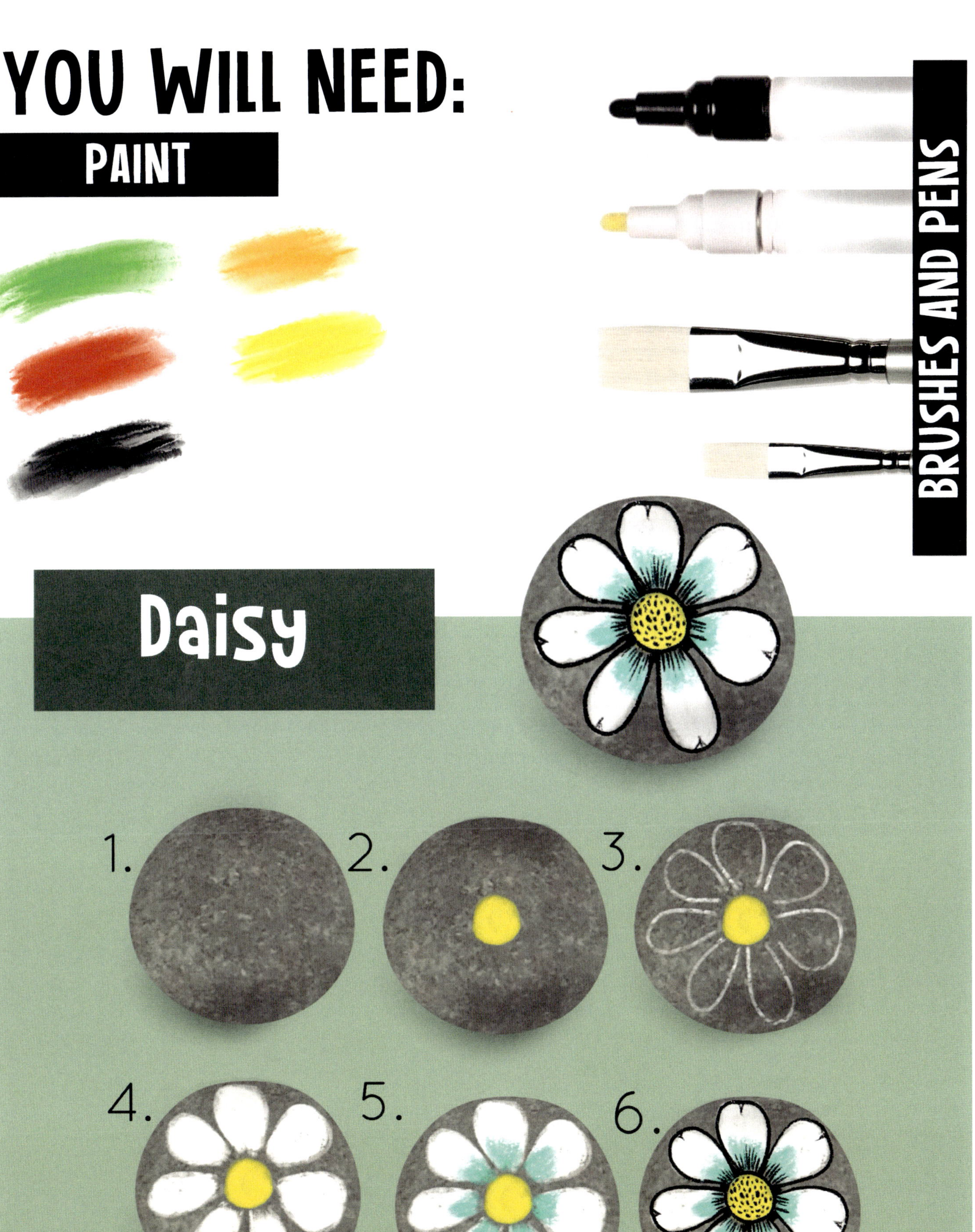

Geometric Leaf

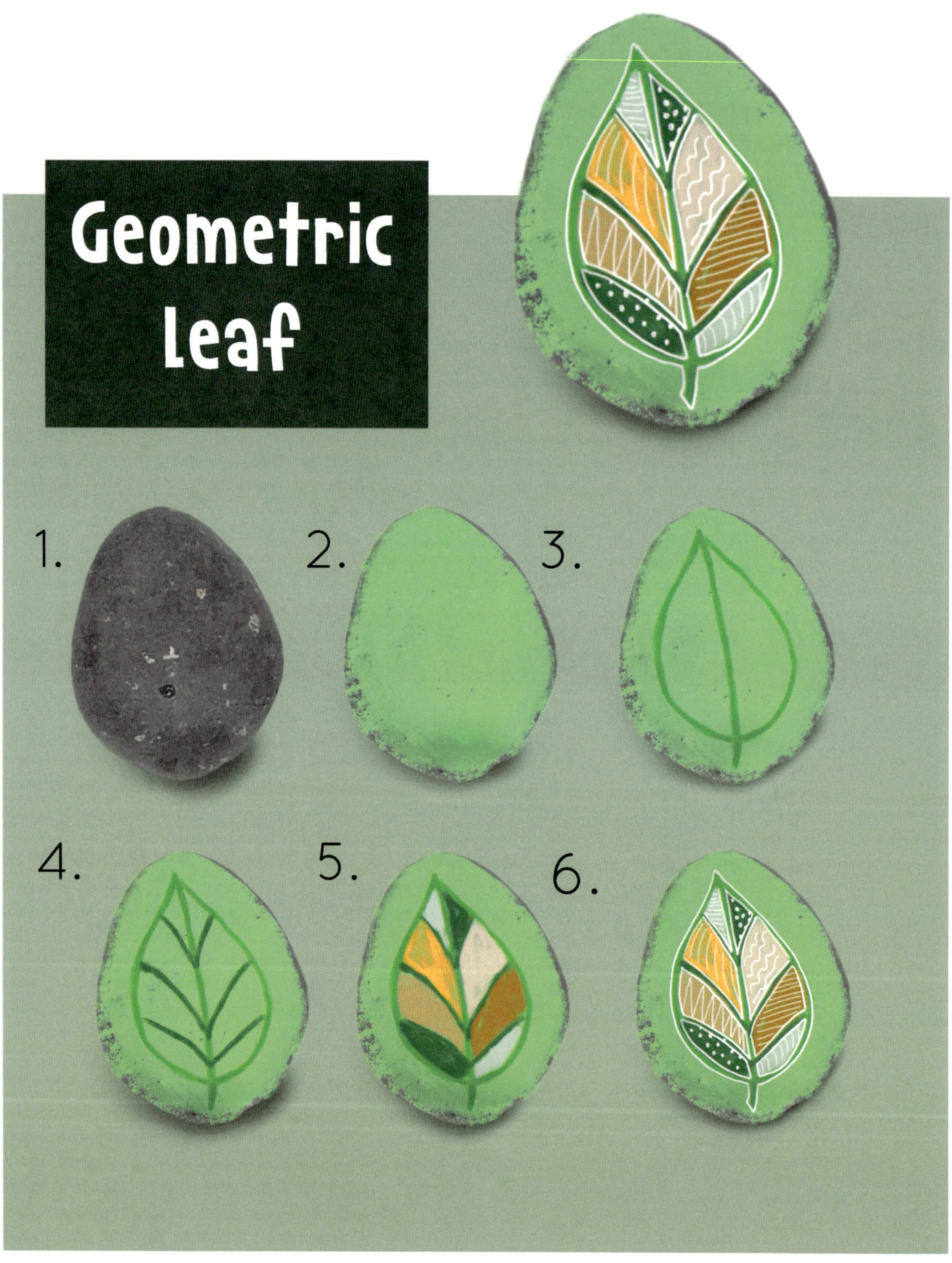

Vine

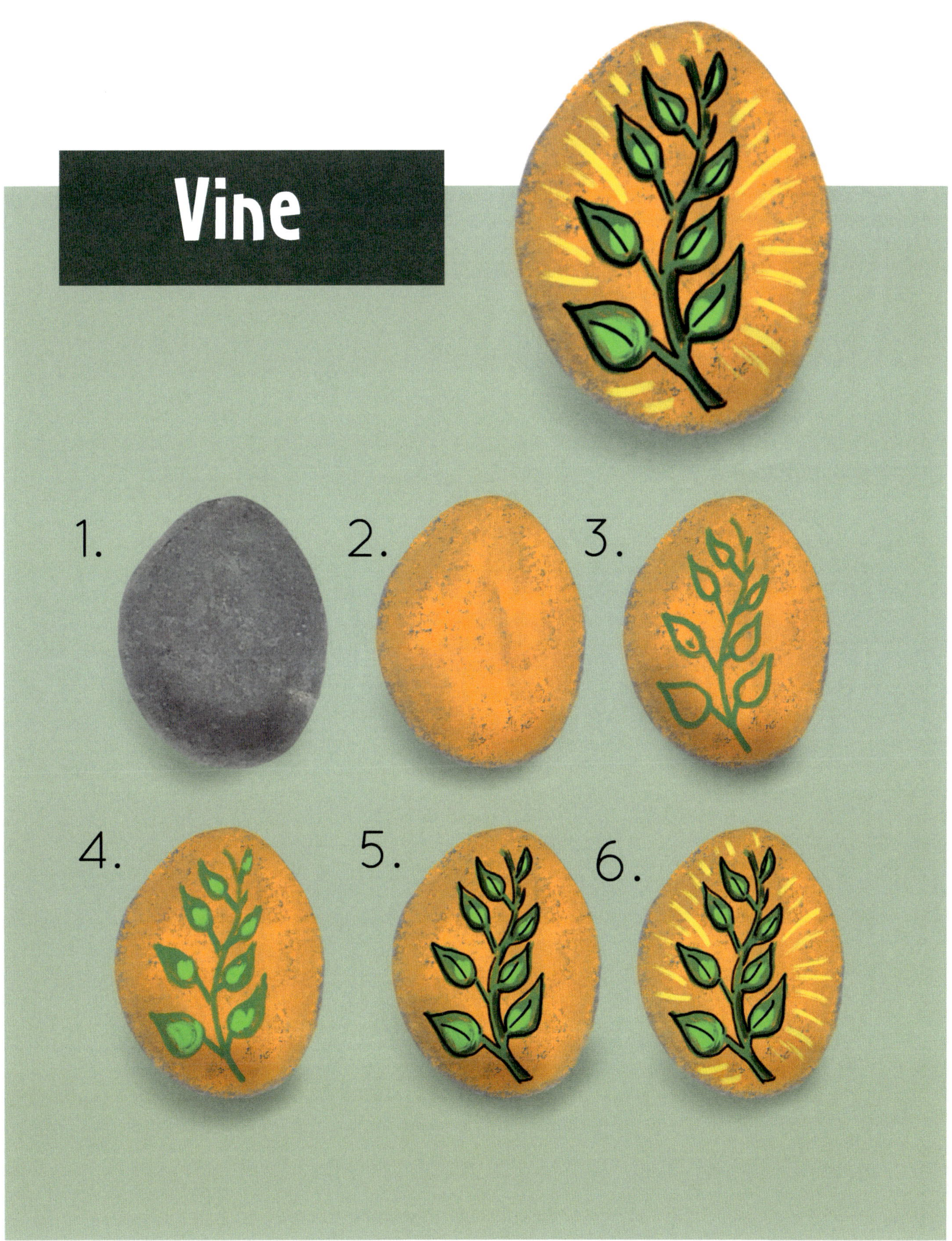

Bouquet

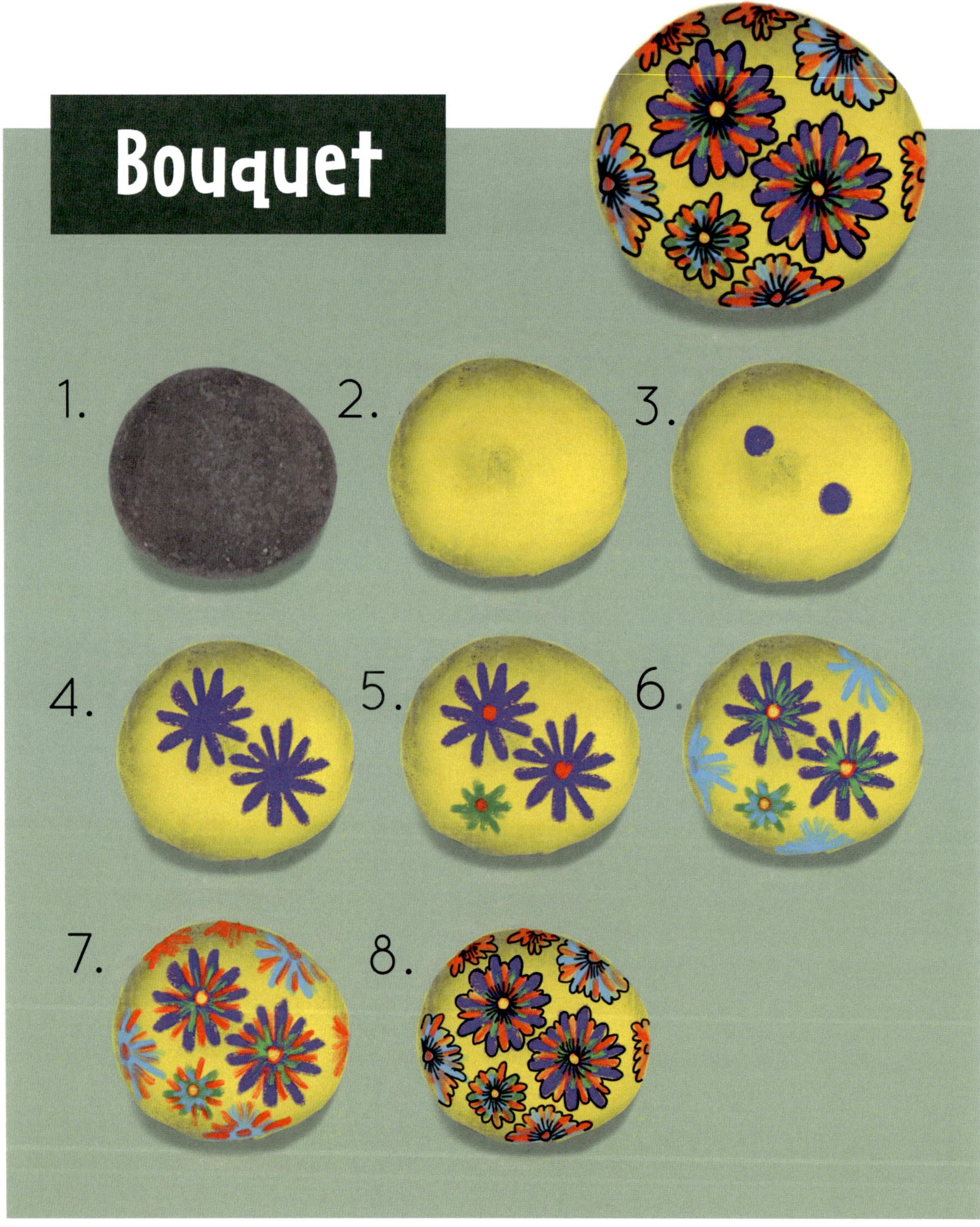

Lotus

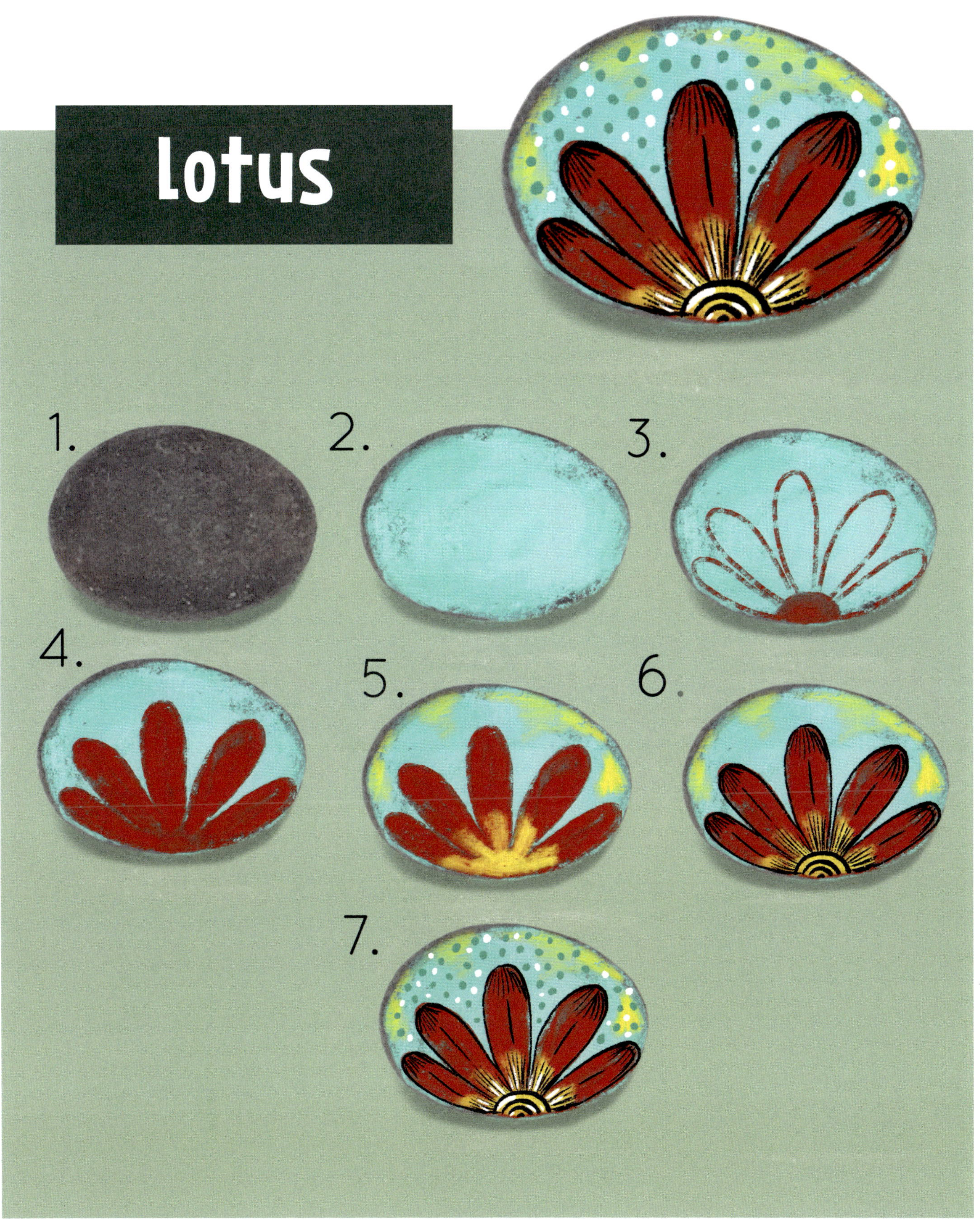

Bugs

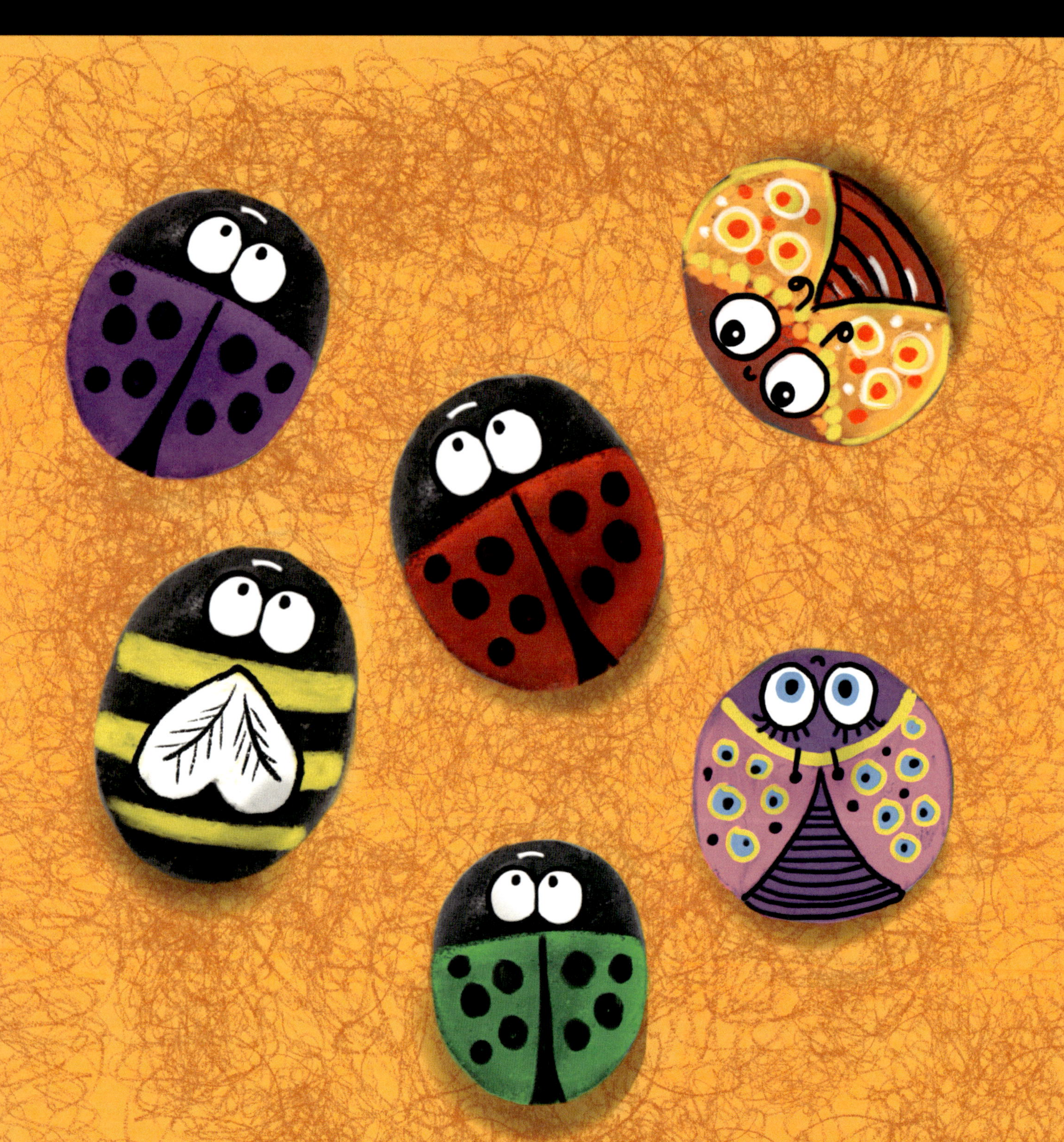

YOU WILL NEED:

PAINT

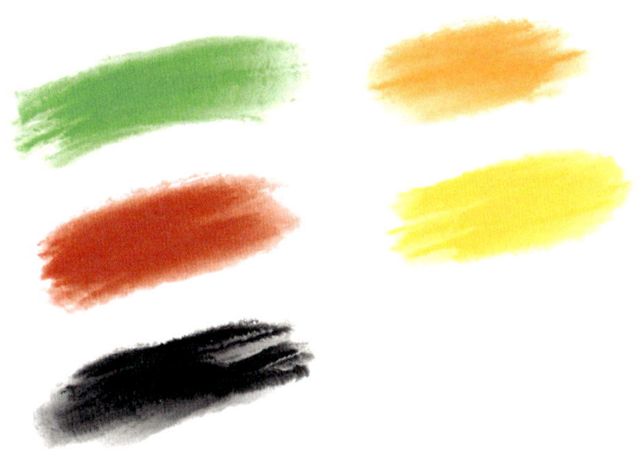

BRUSHES AND PENS

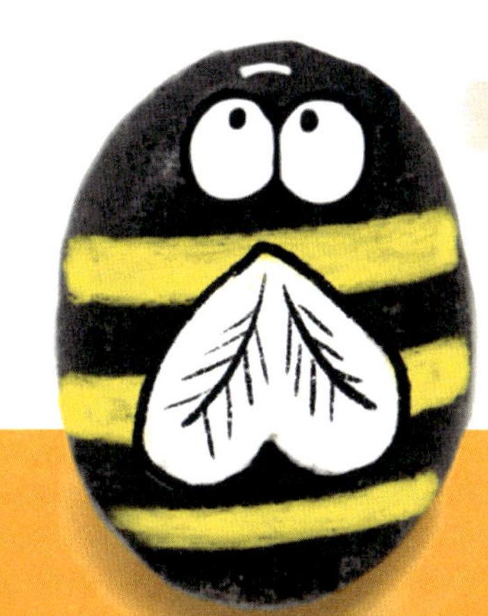

Bumble Bee

1. 2. 3.

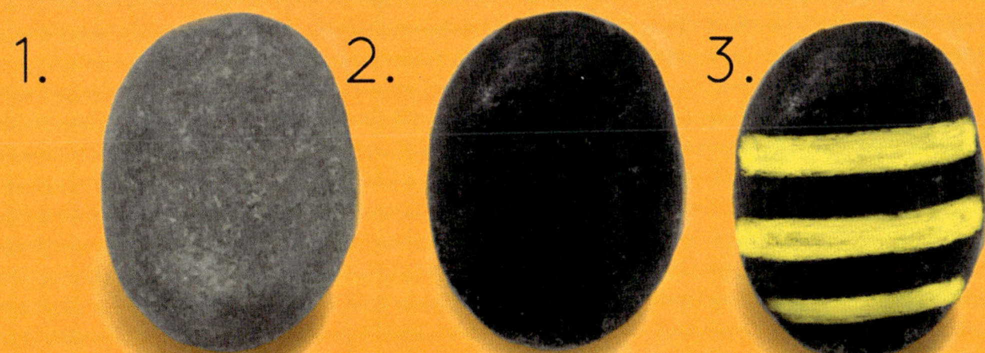

4. 5.

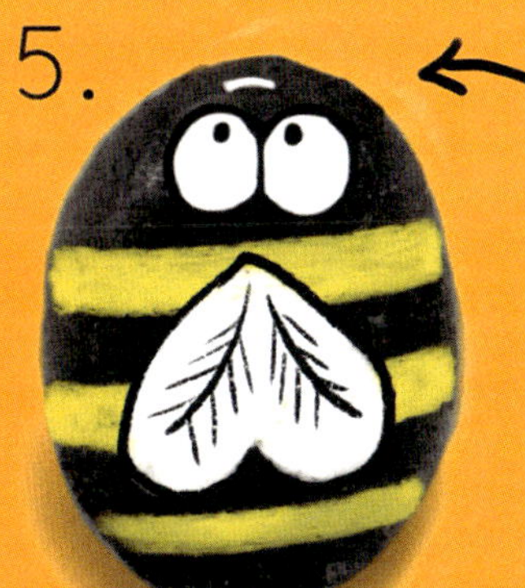

Scribble stickers

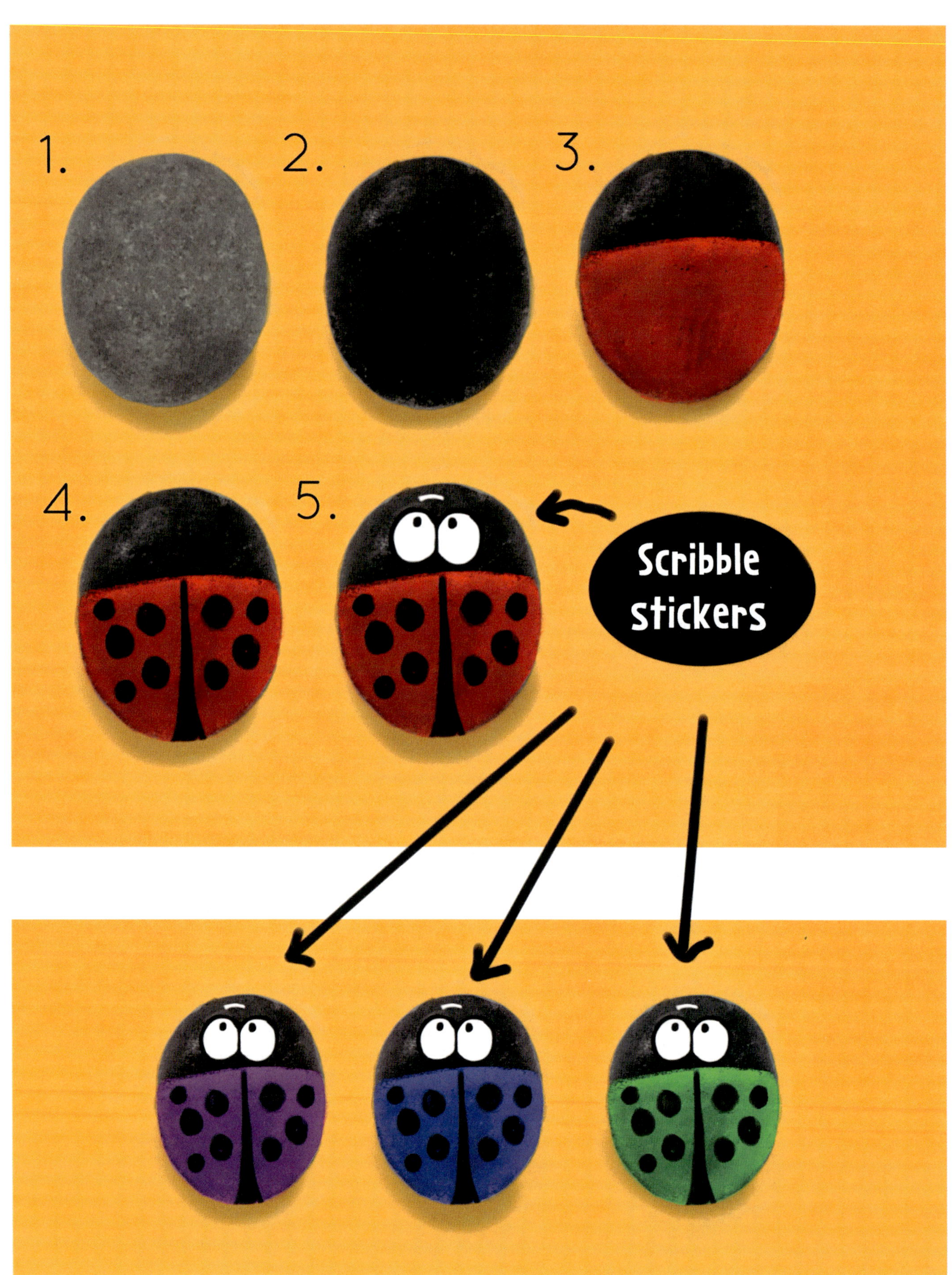
1.
2.
3.
4.
5.
Scribble stickers

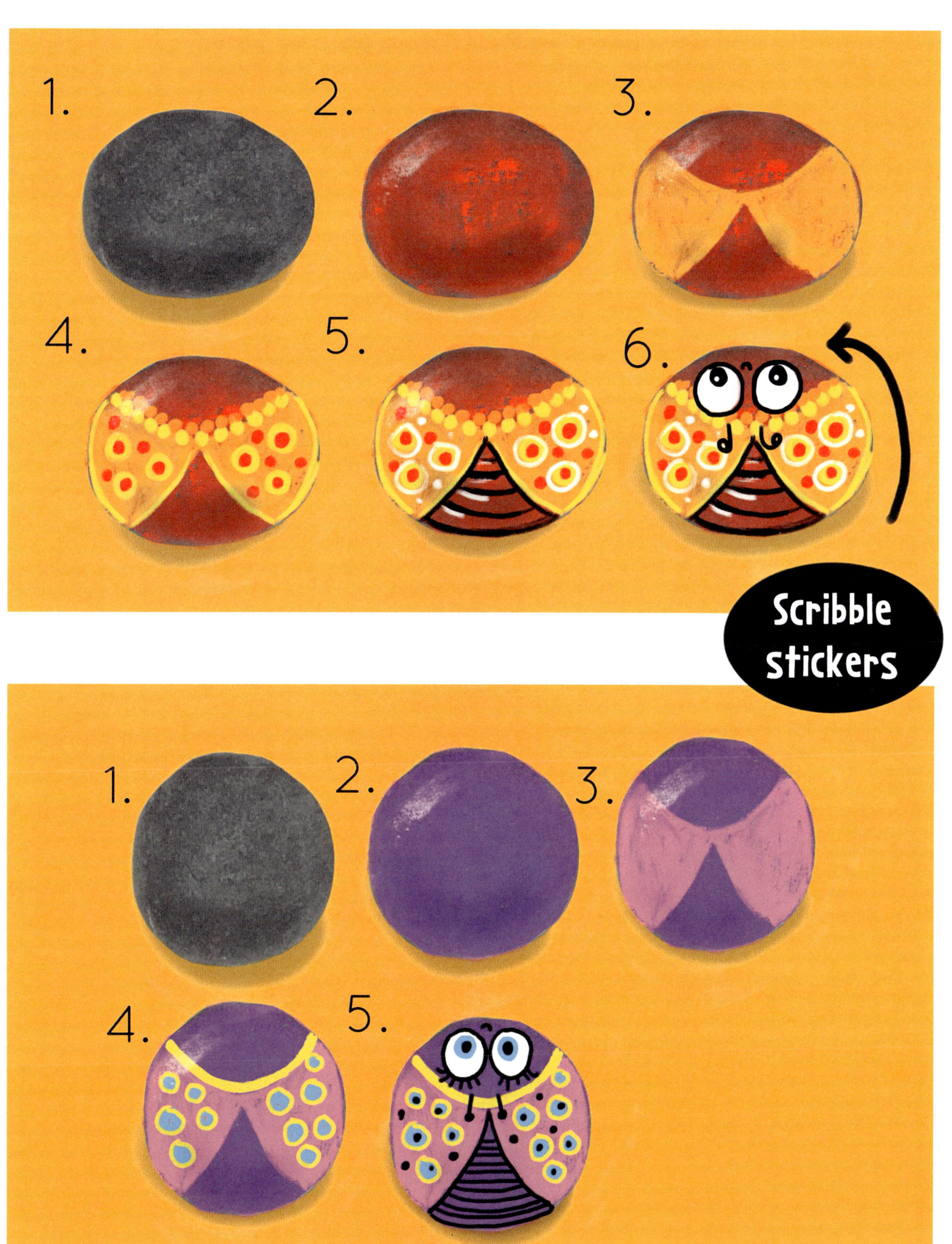
1.
2.
3.
4.
5.
6.
Scribble stickers
1.
2.
3.
4.
5.

Fruit

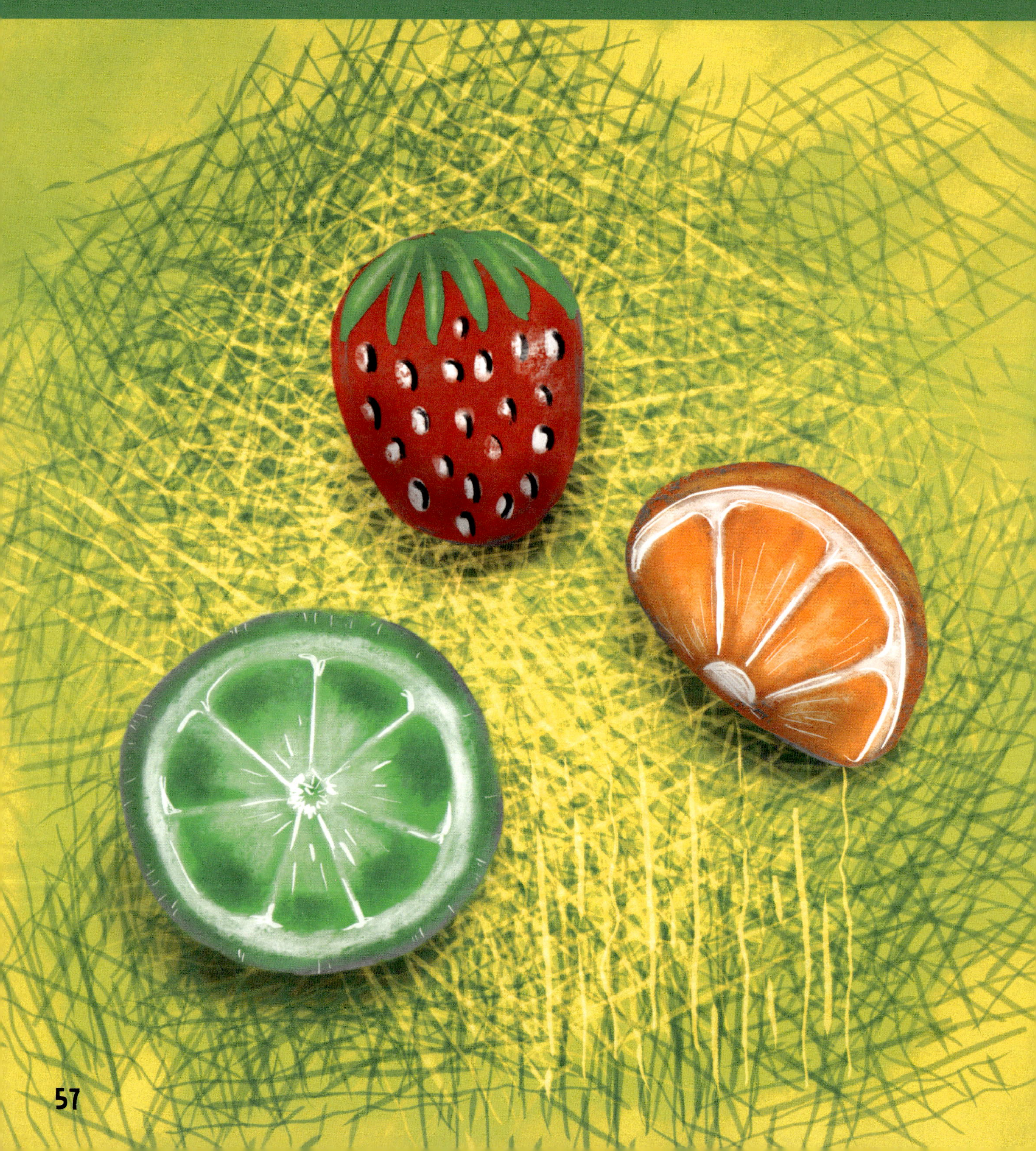

YOU WILL NEED:

PAINT

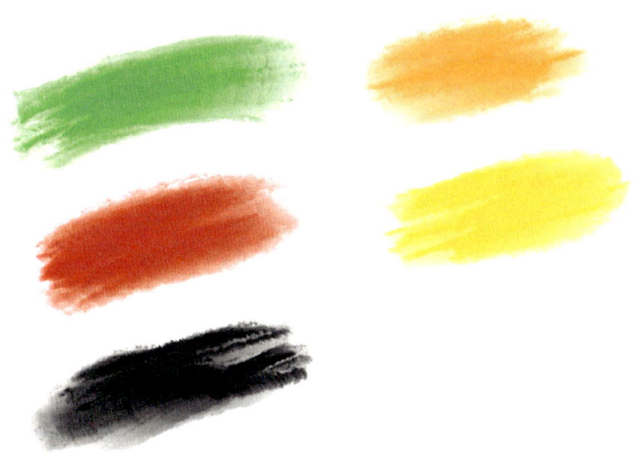

BRUSHES AND PENS

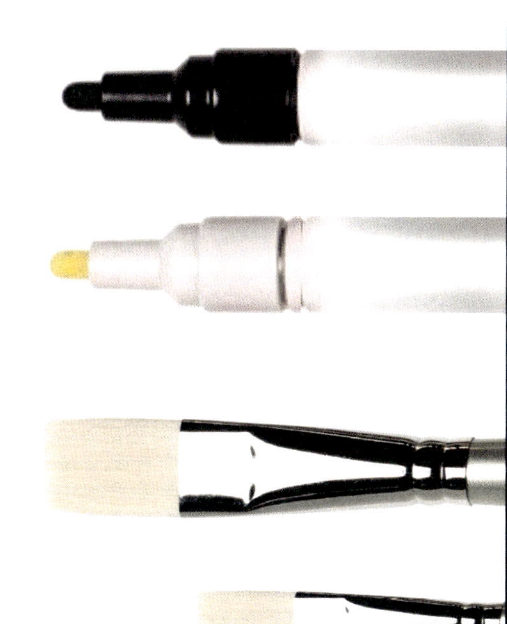

Strawberry

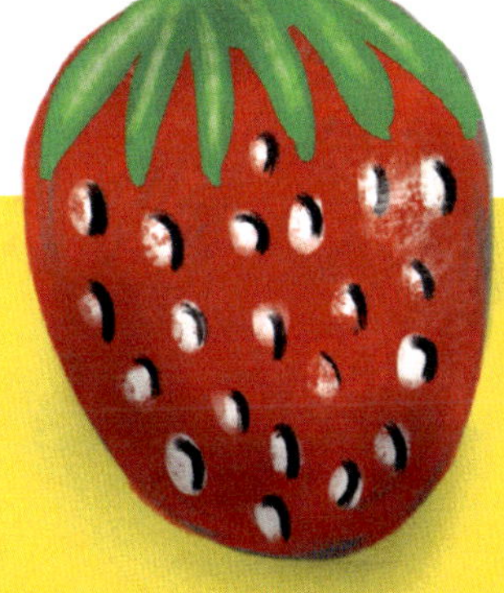

1.

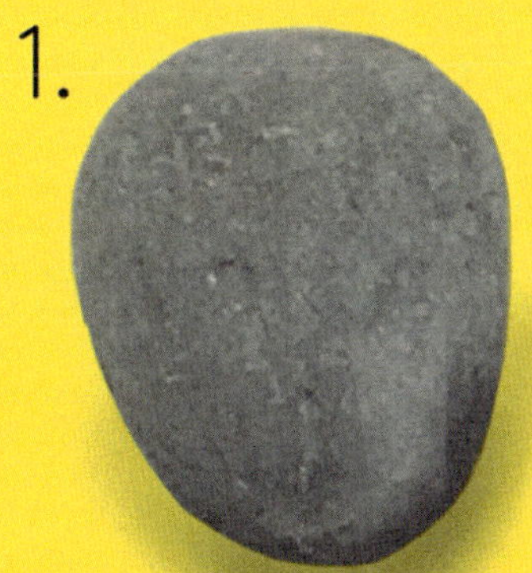

2.

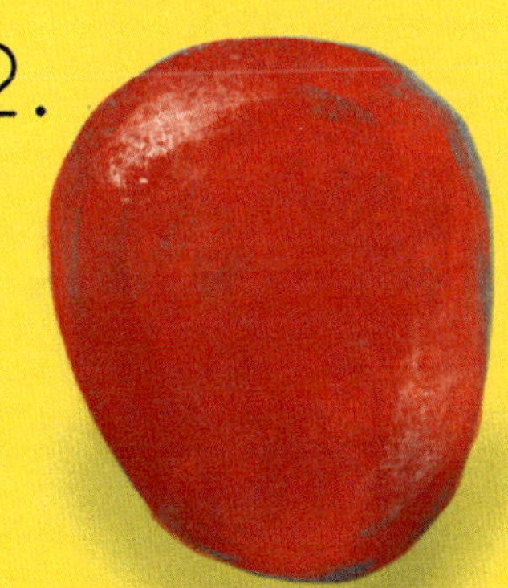

3.

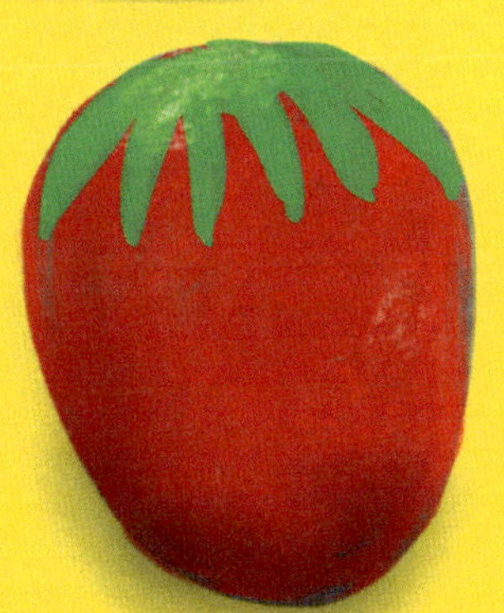

4.

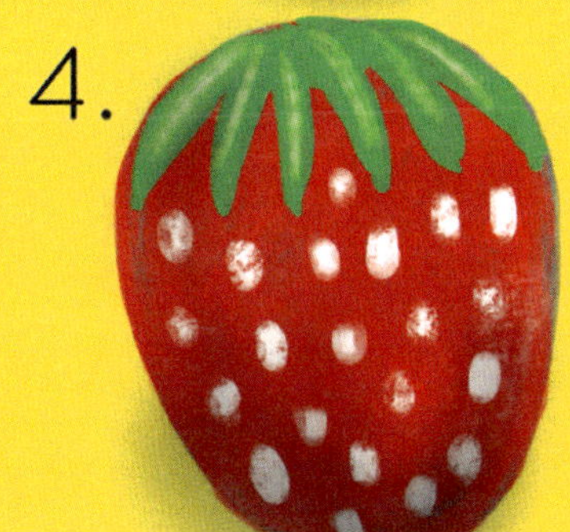

5.

Lime

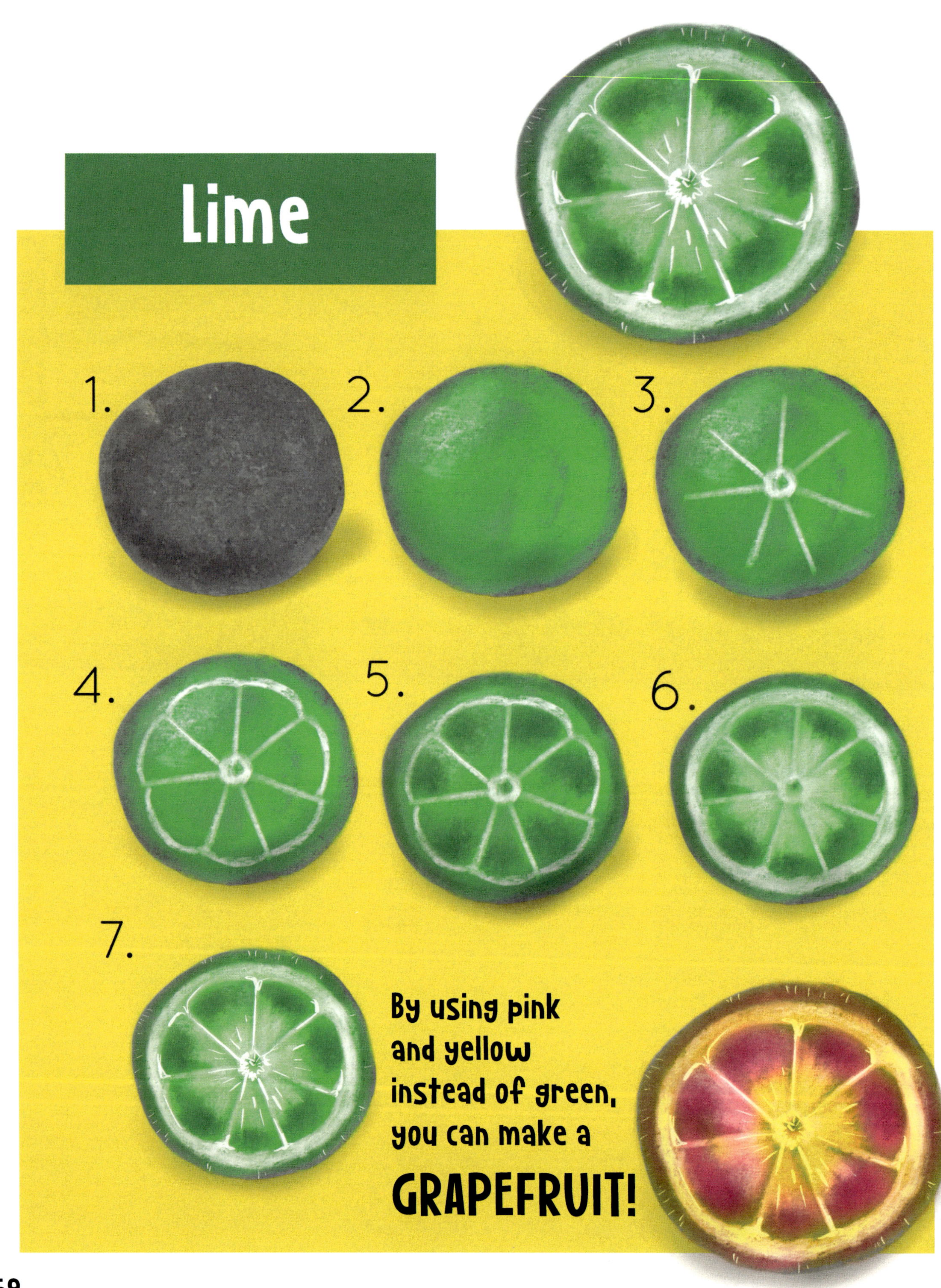

By using pink and yellow instead of green, you can make a **GRAPEFRUIT!**

Orange

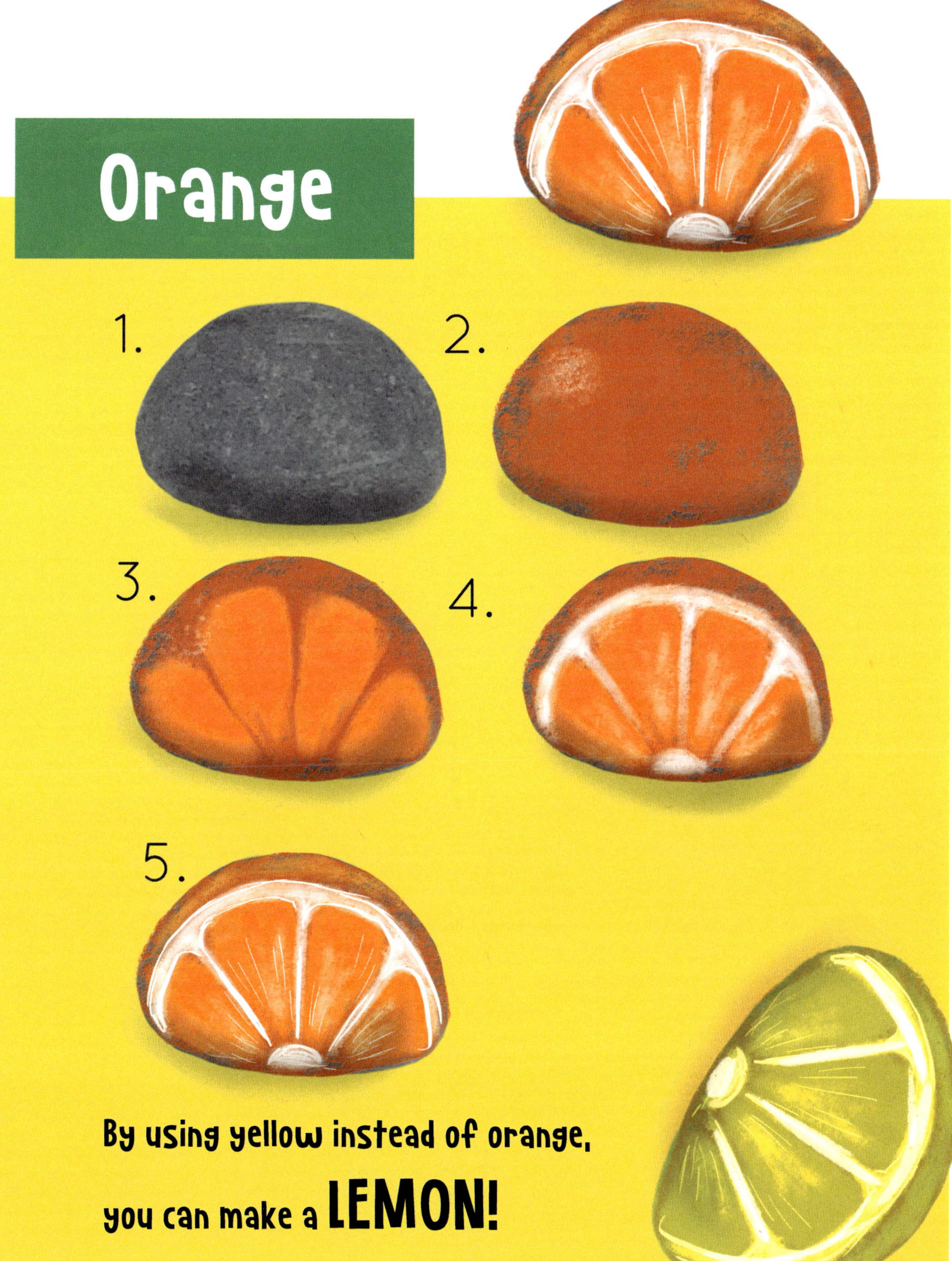

By using yellow instead of orange, you can make a LEMON!

Owls

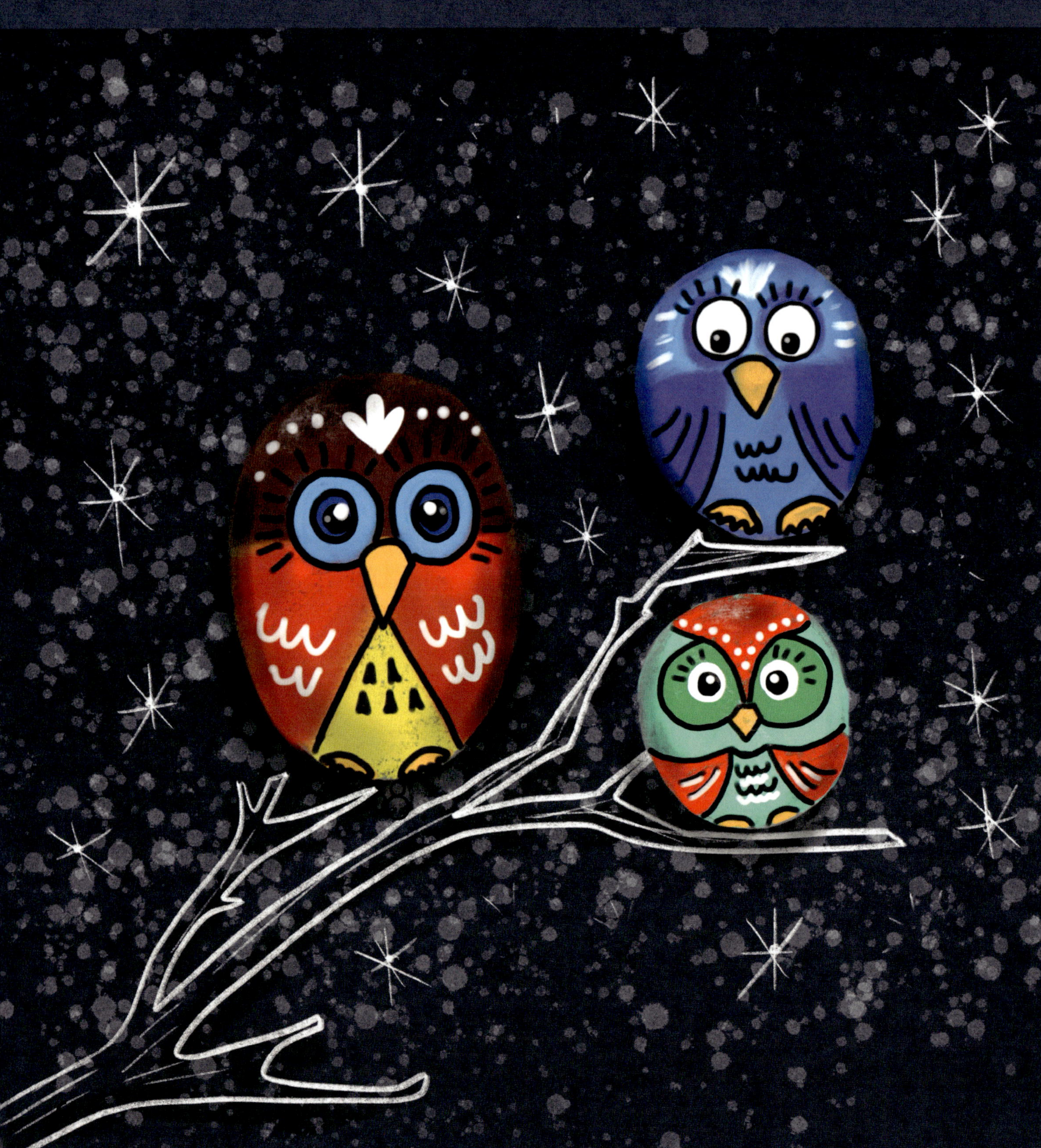

YOU WILL NEED:

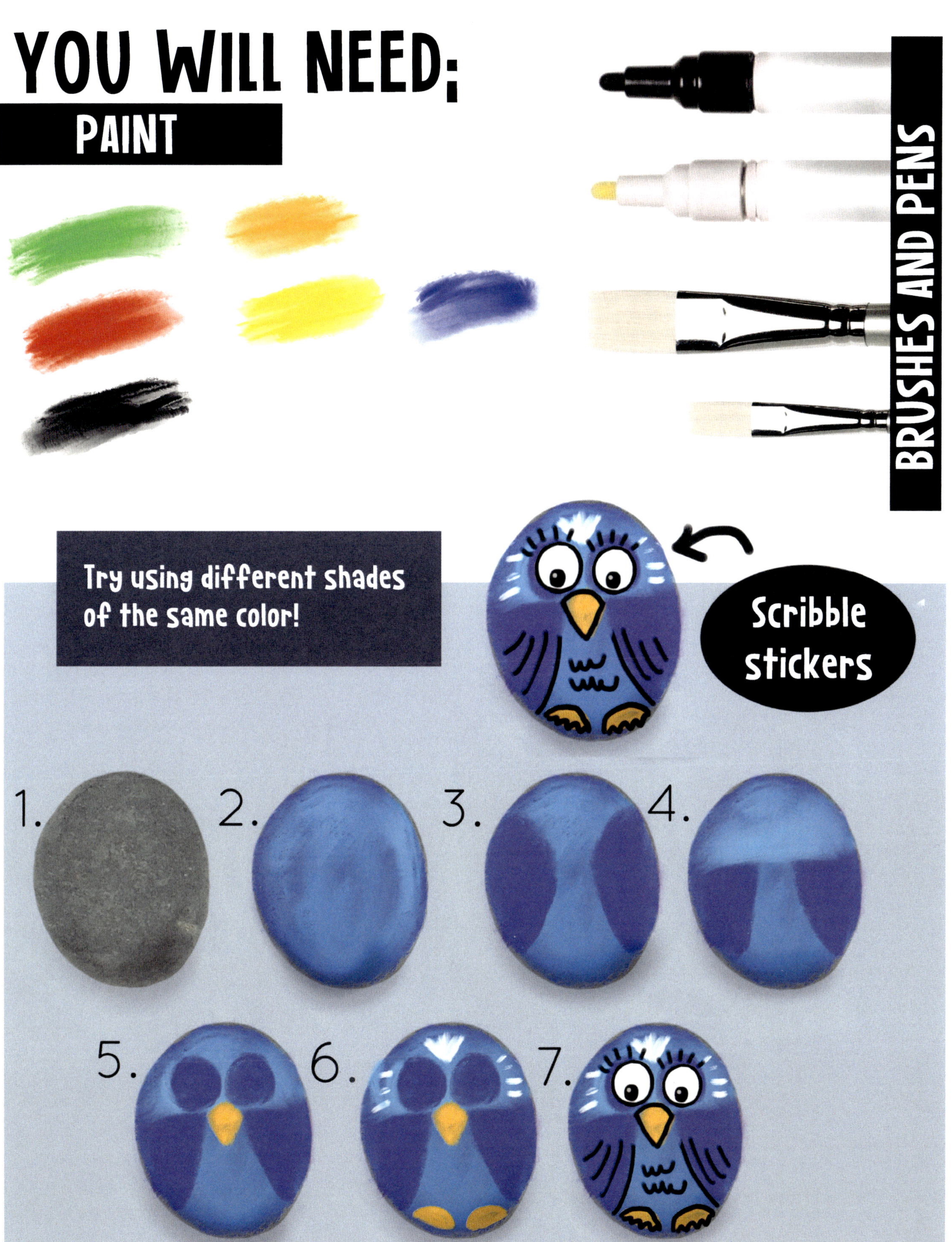

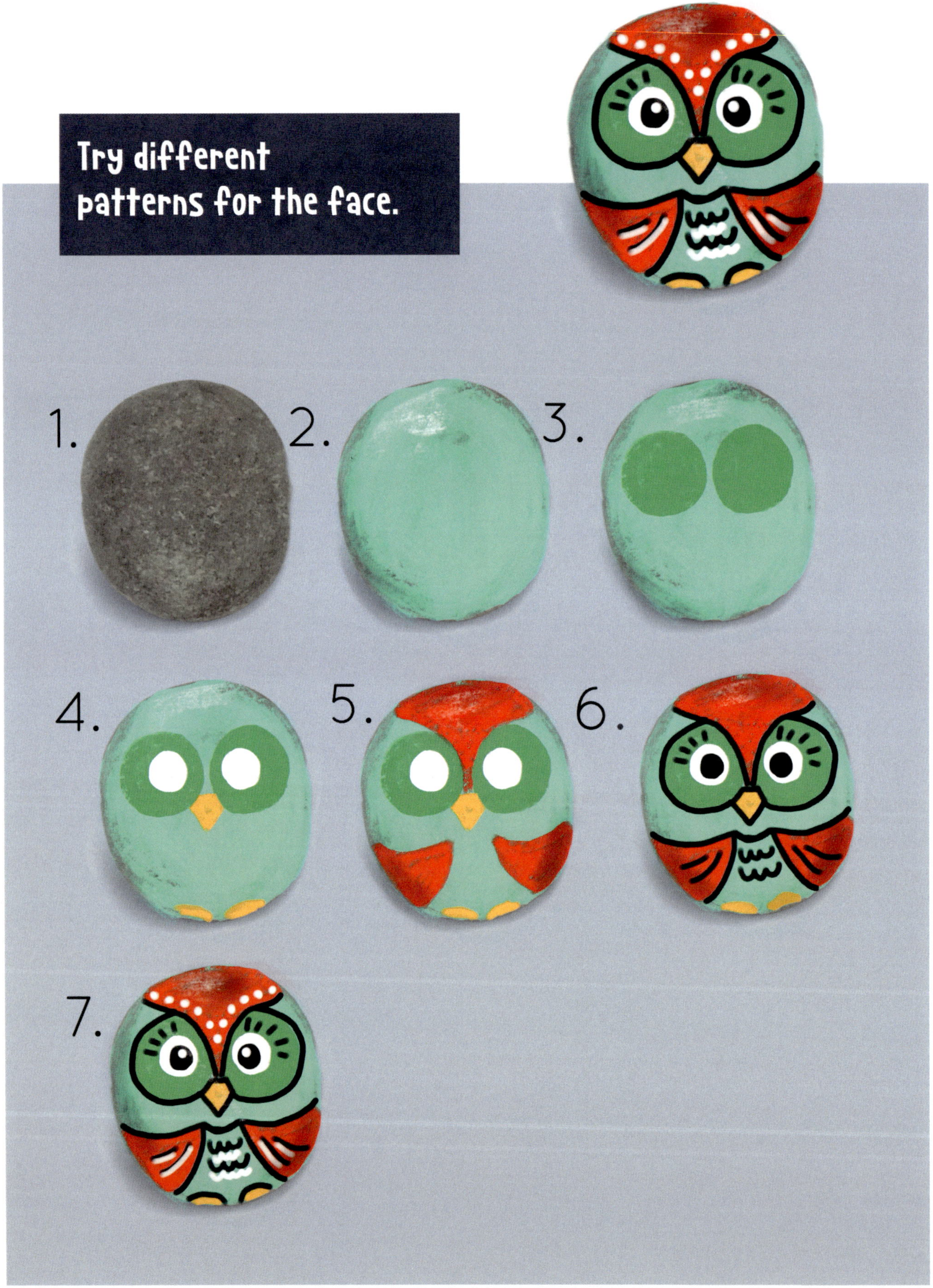
Try different patterns for the face.
1.
2.
3.
4.
5.
6.
7.

Try different patterns for the wings.

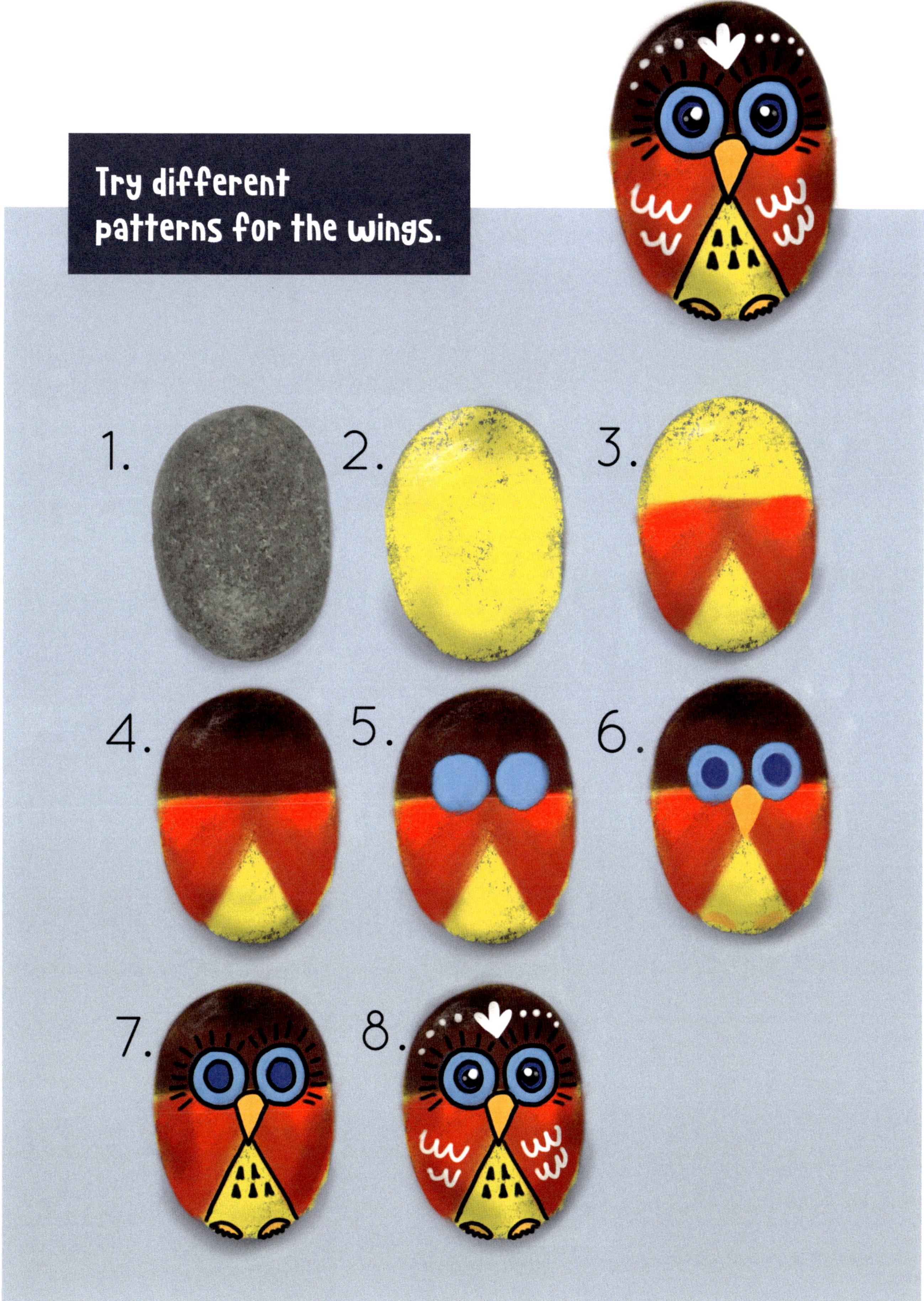

Cityscapes

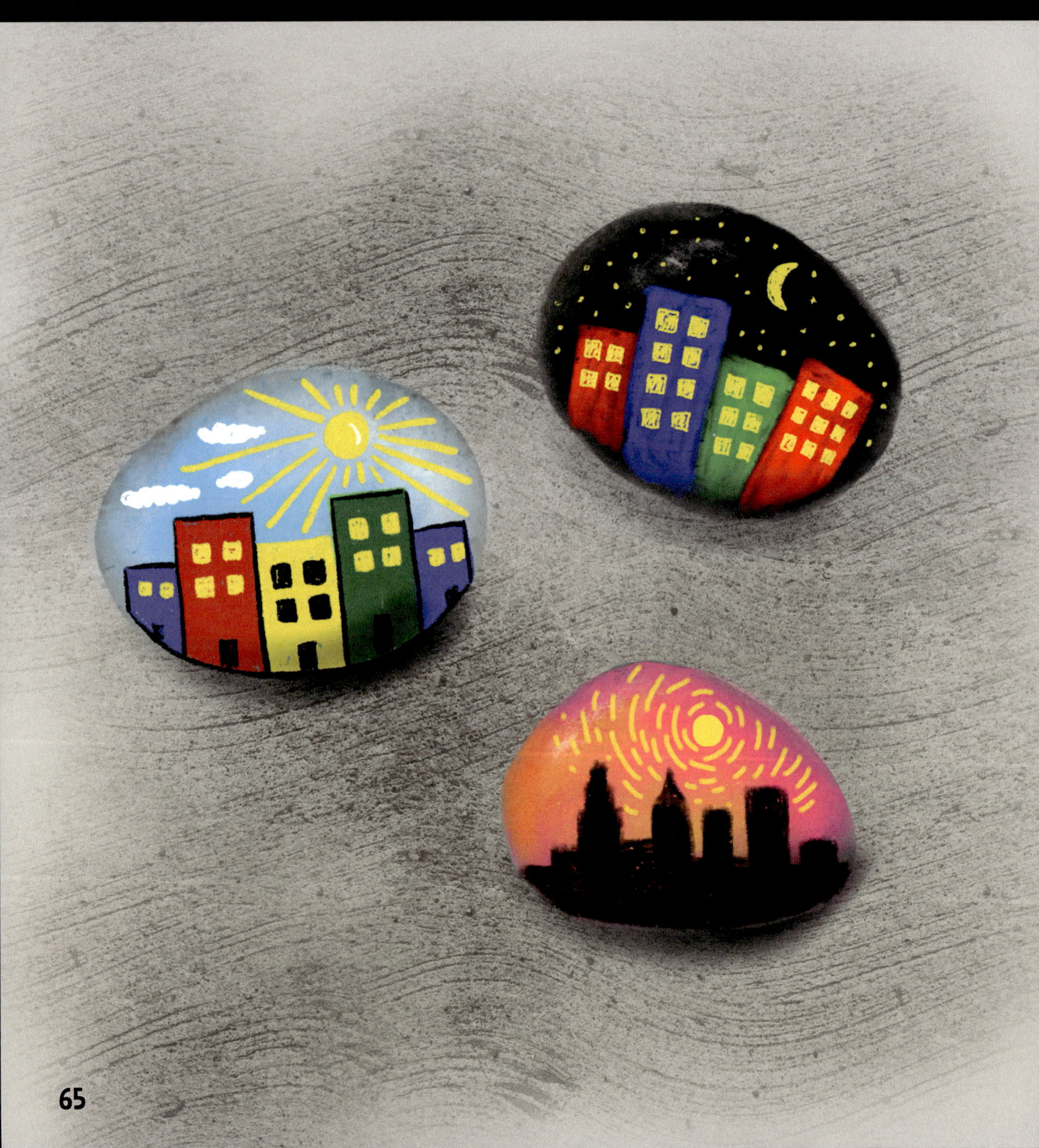

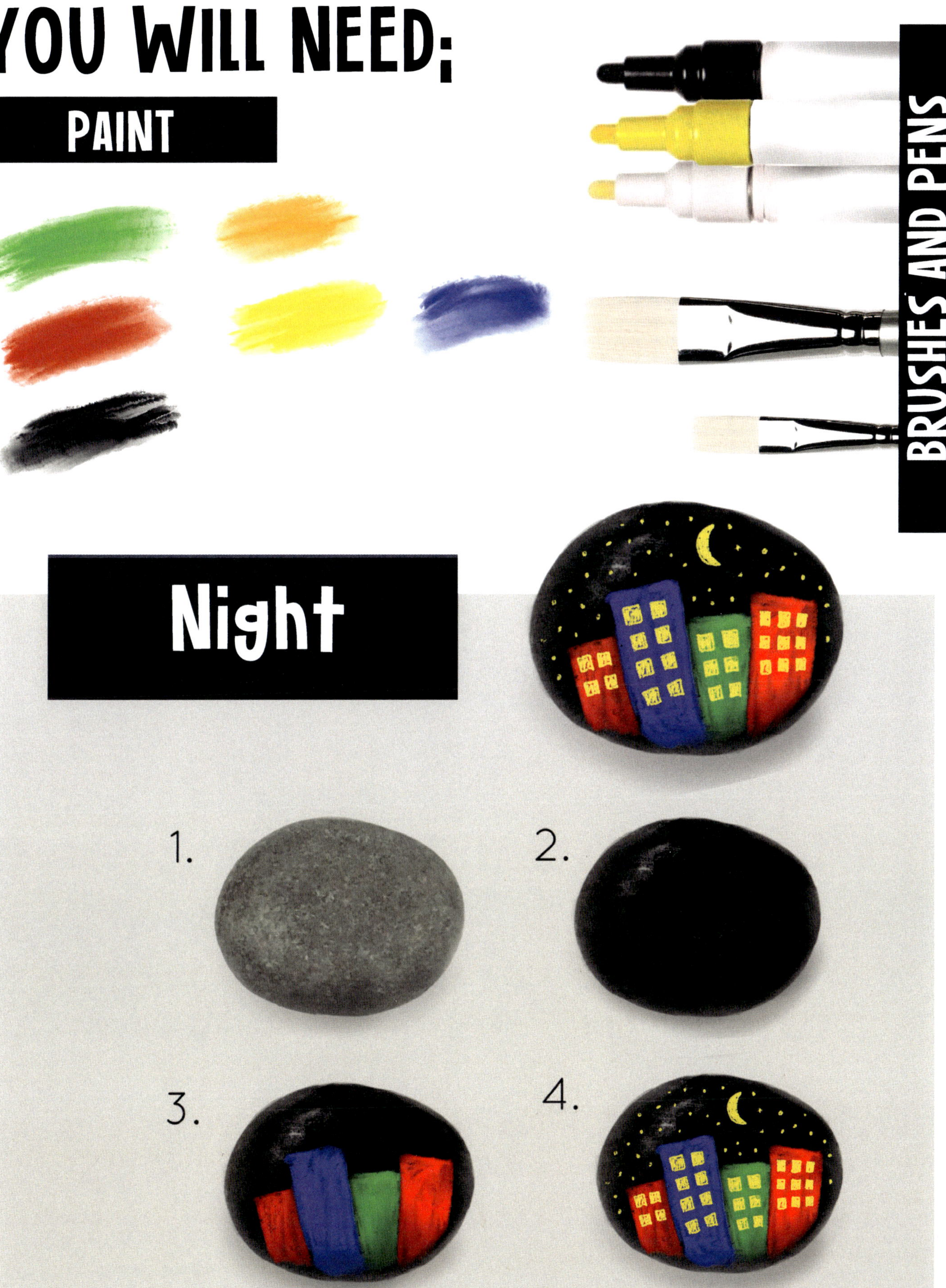
YOU WILL NEED:
PAINT
BRUSHES AND PENS
Night
1.
2.
3.
4.

Sunrise

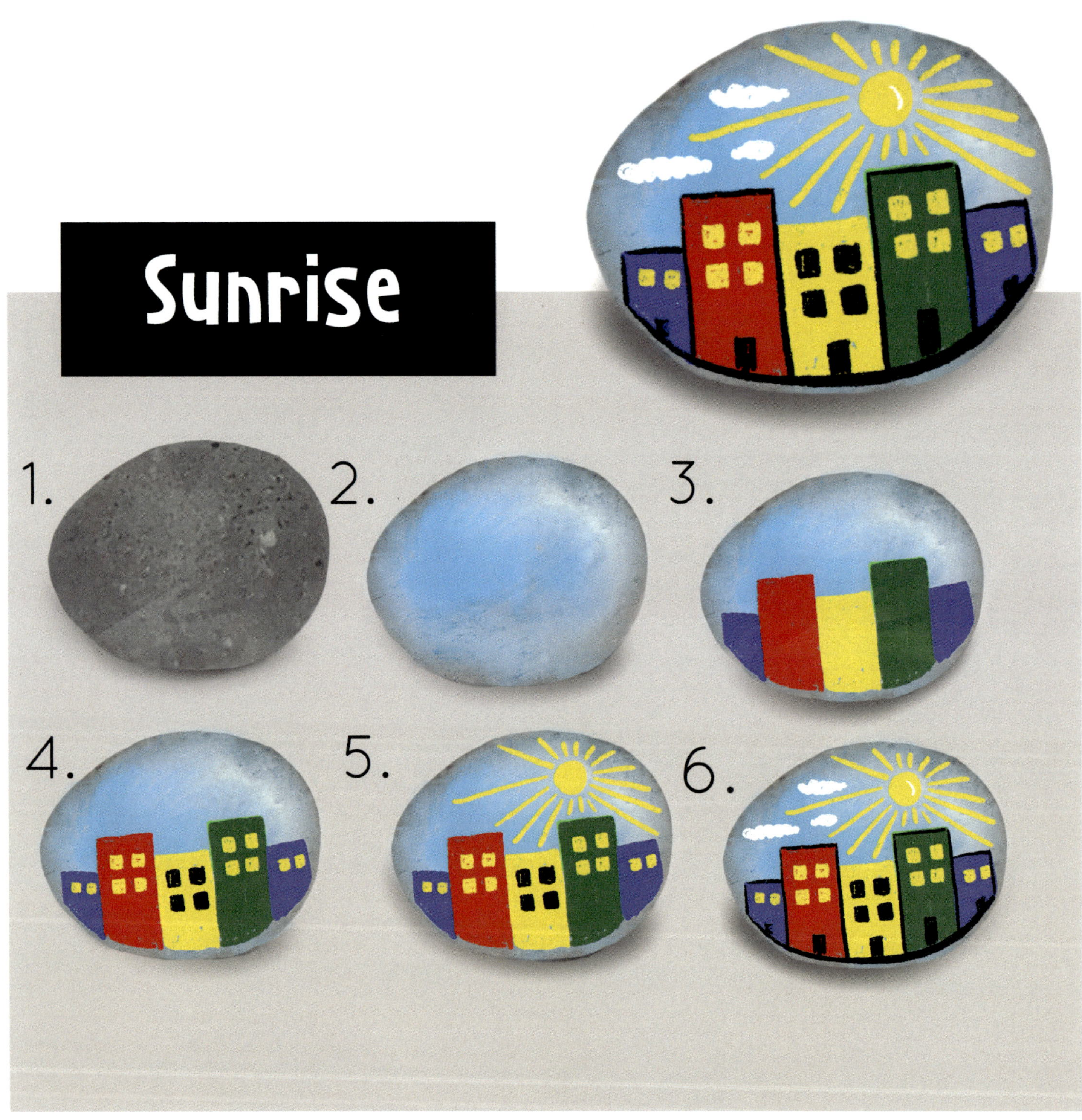

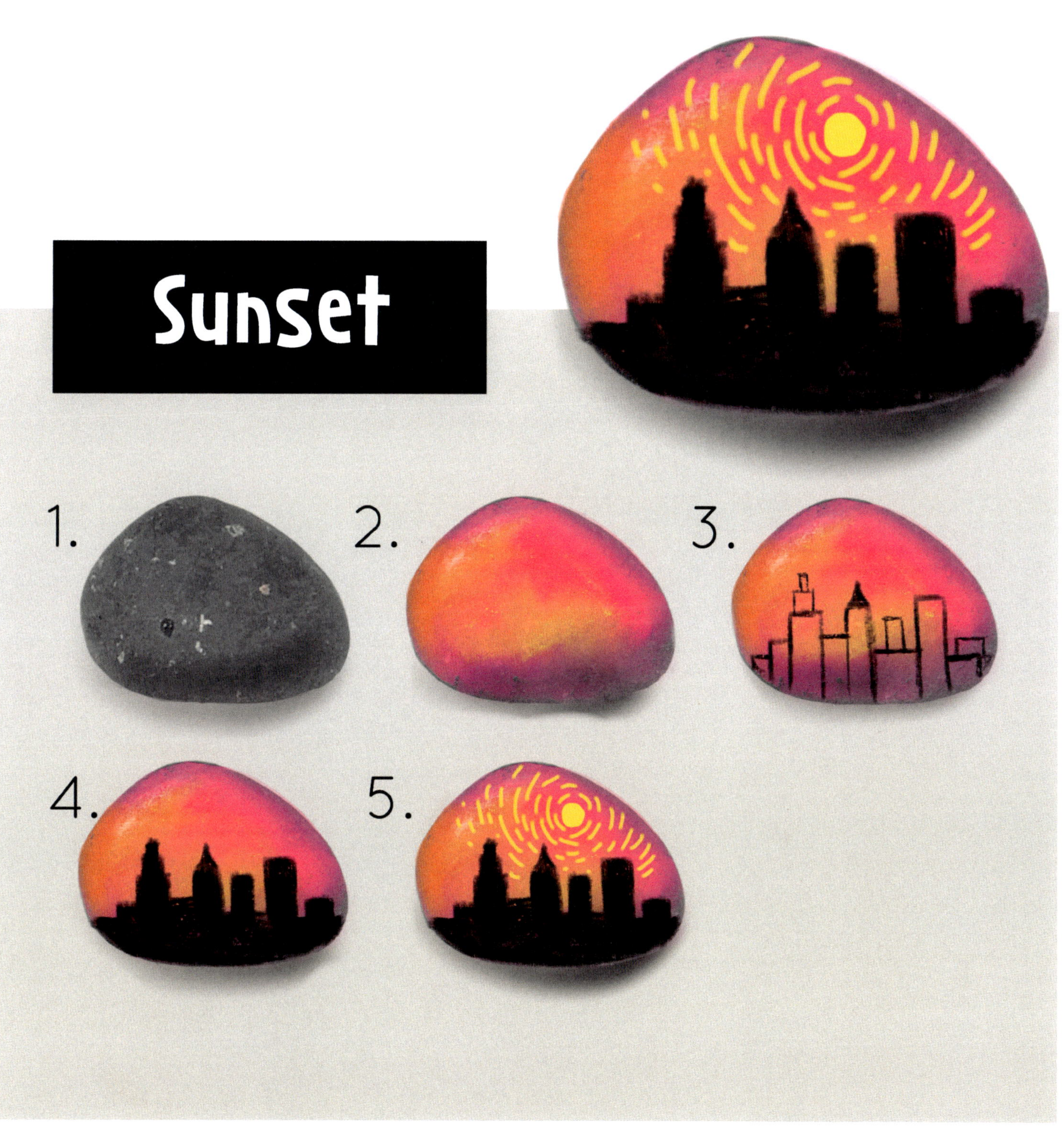
Sunset
1.
2.
3.
4.
5.

After your stone is finished, make sure an adult seals your stone with a clear acrylic sealer or polyurethane spray sealer (to protect from weather and wear).

Planting Rocks

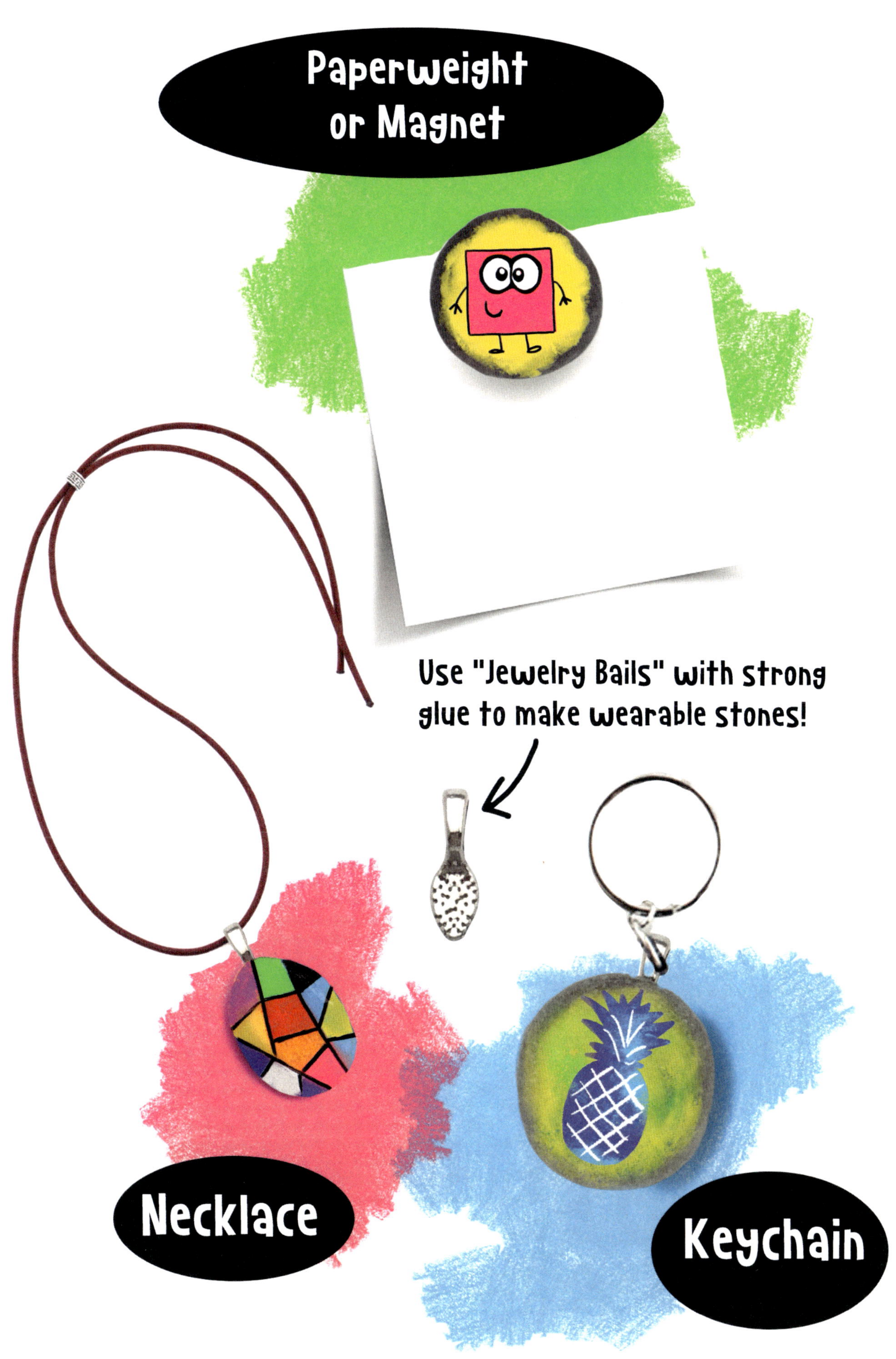
Paperweight or Magnet
Use "Jewelry Bails" with strong glue to make wearable stones!
Necklace
Keychain

Made in the USA
Coppell, TX
29 September 2020

38938191R00045